PRESIDENT'S MALARIA INITIATIVE

Zambia

Malaria Operational Plan FY 2016

TABLE OF CONTENTS

ABBREVIATIONS and ACRONYMS

ACT   Artemisinin-based combination therapy
AIDS   Acquired Immuno-Deficiency Syndrome
AL   Artemether-lumefantrine
ANC   Antenatal care
BCC   Behavior change communication
CDC   Centers for Disease Control and Prevention
CCT   Clinical care teams
CHA   Community health assistant
CHAZ   Churches Health Association of Zambia
CHW   Community health worker
DCHO   District Community Health Office
DCMO   District Community Medical Offices
DDT   Dichloro-diphenyl-trichloroethane
DFID   U.K. Department for International Development
DHA-PQ   Dihydroartemisinin-piperaquine
DHIS2   District Health Information System 2
DHS   Demographic and Health Survey
EMLIP   Essential Medicines Logistics Improvement Program
EPI   Expanded Program on Immunizations
EUV   End-use verification
FANC   Focused antenatal care
FBO   Faith-based organization
FY   Fiscal year
GHI   Global Health Initiative
Global Fund Global Fund to Fight AIDS, Tuberculosis and Malaria
GRZ   Government of the Republic of Zambia
HIV   Human Immunodeficiency Virus
HMIS   Health Management Information System
iCCM   integrated community case management
IEC   Information, education, communication
IMCI   Integrated management of childhood illnesses
IPTp   Intermittent preventive treatment for pregnant women
IRS   Indoor residual spraying
ITN   Insecticide-treated mosquito net
LMU   Logistics Management Unit
M&E   Monitoring and evaluation
MACEPA   Malaria Control and Evaluation Partnership in Africa
MCDMCH   Ministry of Community Development, Mother and Child Health
MIP   Malaria in pregnancy
MIS   Malaria indicator survey
MoH   Ministry of Health
MOP   Malaria Operational Plan
MSL   Medical Stores Limited
NMCC   National Malaria Control Centre

NMCP	National Malaria Control Program
NMSP	National Malaria Strategic Plan
NGO	Non-governmental organization
OPD	Outpatient department
OR	Operational research
OTSS	Outreach training and supportive supervision
PEPFAR	President's Emergency Plan for AIDS Relief
PMI	President's Malaria Initiative
RDT	Rapid diagnostic test
SM&E	Surveillance, monitoring and evaluation
SMAG	Safe Motherhood Action Groups
SP	Sulfadoxine-pyrimethamine
UNDP	United Nations Development Program
UNICEF	United Nations Children's Fund
USAID	United States Agency for International Development
USG	United States Government
WHO	World Health Organization
WHOPES	World Health Organization Pesticide Evaluation Scheme

I. EXECUTIVE SUMMARY

When it was launched in 2005, the goal of the President's Malaria Initiative (PMI) was to reduce malaria-related mortality by 50% across 15 high-burden countries in sub-Saharan Africa through a rapid scale-up of four proven and highly effective malaria prevention and treatment measures: insecticide-treated mosquito nets (ITNs); indoor residual spraying (IRS); accurate diagnosis and prompt treatment with artemisinin-based combination therapies (ACTs); and intermittent preventive treatment for pregnant women (IPTp). With the passage of the Tom Lantos and Henry J. Hyde Global Leadership against HIV/AIDS, Tuberculosis, and Malaria Act in 2008, PMI developed a U.S. Government Malaria Strategy for 2009–2014. This strategy included a long-term vision for malaria control in which sustained high coverage with malaria prevention and treatment interventions would progressively lead to malaria-free zones in Africa, with the ultimate goal of worldwide malaria eradication by 2040-2050. Consistent with this strategy and the increase in annual appropriations supporting PMI, four new sub-Saharan African countries and one regional program in the Greater Mekong Subregion of Southeast Asia were added in 2011. The contributions of PMI, together with those of other partners, have led to dramatic improvements in the coverage of malaria control interventions in PMI-supported countries, and all 15 original countries have documented substantial declines in all-cause mortality rates among children less than five years of age.

In 2015, PMI launched the next six-year strategy, setting forth a bold and ambitious goal and objectives. The PMI Strategy for 2015-2020 takes into account the progress over the past decade and the new challenges that have arisen. Malaria prevention and control remains a major U.S. foreign assistance objective and PMI's Strategy fully aligns with the U.S. Government's vision of ending preventable child and maternal deaths and ending extreme poverty. It is also in line with the goals articulated in the draft RBM Partnership's second Global Malaria Action Plan and WHO's draft Global Technical Strategy. Under the PMI Strategy for 2015-2020, the U.S. Government's goal is to work with PMI-supported countries and partners to further reduce malaria deaths and substantially decrease malaria morbidity, towards the long-term goal of elimination.

Zambia was selected as a PMI focus country in FY 2007.

This Fiscal Year (FY) 2016 Malaria Operational Plan presents a detailed implementation plan for Zambia, based on the strategies of PMI and the National Malaria Control Program (NMCP). It was developed in consultation with the NMCP and with the participation of national and international partners involved in malaria prevention and control in the country. The activities that PMI is proposing to support fit in well with the National Malaria Control Strategic Plan (NMSP) and build on investments made by PMI and other partners to improve and expand malaria-related services, including the Global Fund to Fight AIDS, Tuberculosis, and Malaria (Global Fund) malaria grants. This document briefly reviews the current status of malaria control policies and interventions in Zambia, describes progress to date, identifies challenges and unmet needs to achieving the targets of the NMCP and PMI, and provides a description of activities that are planned with FY 2016 funding.

The proposed FY 2016 PMI budget for Zambia is $24 million. PMI will support the following intervention areas with these funds:

Insecticide-treated nets (ITNs):

To achieve the goal for universal net coverage, a rolling mass distribution campaign was conducted during a period of 18 months to distribute over 8 million ITNs nationwide. The mass distribution campaign was a collaborative effort between the NMCP, PMI, Global Fund, DFID, UNDP, and other partners. The campaign started in Western Province and Copperbelt in FY 2014. Mass campaigns also occurred in rural districts of Lusaka Province in FY 2014, as well as in selected districts in Eastern Province. In FY 2015, mass campaigns occurred in Eastern, Central, Northwestern, Southern, Muchinga, Northern, and Luapula Provinces. PMI provided enough ITNs to assure universal coverage in Luapula. Global Fund/UNDP supported the remaining six provinces. Within the Global Fund/UNDP-supported districts, PMI provided ITNs to top up the campaigns in Copperbelt and rural districts of Lusaka province. PMI also supports routine ITN distribution systems in Zambia through ANC and EPI clinics, as well as through the expansion of routine distribution channels to include school-based and community-based distribution. PMI also supported operational research to examine the durability of ITNs to guide decisions about net replacement. With FY 2016 funding, PMI will focus on the procurement and distribution of ITNs for the 2017 mass distribution campaign. In addition, PMI will support continuous distribution through ANC/EPI, as well as providing support to rollout school-based and community channels. PMI will continue to monitor the durability of ITNs distributed during the 2013/2014 mass campaign. In order to maximize ITN usage, PMI will continue to support BCC activities, prioritizing local over national activities.

Indoor residual spraying (IRS):

In FY 2015, PMI supported the NMCP Indoor Residual Spraying (IRS) operations in 25 PMI focus districts (9 in Eastern Province, 7 in Muchinga Province and 9 in Northern Province). PMI supported an additional 15 districts, with funding from DFID (11 in Luapula and 4 in Central Province). Approximately 409,544 structures were sprayed using organophosphate insecticide, out of the targeted 438,252 structures (93% coverage) protecting more than 2 million people (approximately 10% of the Zambian population). DFID support for IRS in the 15 districts will culminate at the end of calendar year 2015. The MOH committed significant funding towards IRS in 2014. With funding from the Zambian government, the NMCP conducted IRS in 43 non-PMI supported districts using organophosphates. The NMCP has sufficient insecticides left over from the 2014 spraying season to use in the 43 districts during the 2015 spray season. In 2014, PMI supported piloting of targeted IRS in 15 districts, 11 in Luapula and 4 in Central Province. Targeting involves enumeration of IRS eligible structures using satellite mapping and targeting IRS using HMIS data. In 2015, targeted IRS will continue in Luapula and Central Province. With FY 2016 funding, PMI will cover the cost of IRS in up to 36 districts in 5 provinces: Central, Eastern, Luapula, Muchinga, and Northern. Approximately 400,000 structures will be targeted protecting more than 2 million people.

Malaria in pregnancy (MIP):

The NMCP updated their recommendations for IPTp to recommend sulfadoxine-pyrimethamine (SP) at the sixteenth week of gestation, with subsequent doses at every monthly visit given up to the time of delivery, in accordance with recent changes in the World Health Organization (WHO) recommendations. PMI supports three main strategies to address malaria in pregnancy: IPTp, ITNs, and case management. The 73% national coverage of two doses of IPTp obscures substantially lower rates in rural areas and among poorer women. Two major barriers to increasing three-dose IPTp coverage are late attendance of women for ANC and stockouts of SP. Because the availability of SP is critical for IPTp, PMI continues to invest in the Essential Medicines Logistics Improvement Program (EMLIP) to improve distribution of malaria commodities. PMI also supported training of provincial- and district-level clinical care teams in providing supervision for IPTp, training of healthcare workers in IPTp, and behavior change communication (BCC) activities to encourage early and frequent ANC attendance to receive IPTp. With FY 2016 funding, PMI will support supervision and training of health workers in the new NMCP guidelines for IPTp and BCC activities related to malaria in pregnancy.

Case management:

Diagnosis and Treatment

NMCP Guidelines for the Diagnosis and Treatment of Malaria in Zambia recommend parasitological diagnosis for all suspected malaria cases where confirmatory capacity is available. Diagnostic availability has increased over the past year with the procurement of over 17 million rapid diagnostic tests (RDTs) in 2014. The Government of the Republic of Zambia (GRZ) procured over 5.6 million RDTs. In addition PMI, DFID, and CHAZ supported procurement and distribution of 3.5 million, over 7 million, and 243,000 RDTs respectively. In 2015, PMI procured over 1.6 million RDTs and reagents and supplies for microscopy. PMI also supported the training of clinical and laboratory personnel in the use of diagnostic tools, and training of national, provincial, and district level staff in providing outreach training and support supervision (OTSS) for quality assurance of malaria diagnostics. With FY 2016 funding, PMI will procure 3 million RDTs and reagents and supplies for microscopy. PMI will continue to strengthen OTSS of health workers, together with quality control of laboratory diagnosis.

In 2014, the NMCP and partners made revisions to the *Guidelines for the Diagnosis and Treatment of Malaria in Zambia* that included: injectable artesunate for severe malaria, dihydroartemisinin-piperaquine (DHA-PQ) as an alternate first-line treatment of uncomplicated malaria, and rectal artesunate for pre-referral treatment of severe malaria. PMI procured approximately 3.5 million ACTs in 2014 for the treatment of malaria in health facilities and in the community. In addition, 3.5 million ACTs were procured with DFID funding (using PMI's procurement mechanism). The GRZ procured over 11 million ACT treatments. In 2014 there was no national level stockout of RDTs or ACTs reported in the country. In 2015 approximately 20 million ACT treatments are expected, with PMI providing over 4 million treatments and the GRZ providing over 8.9 million treatments. If all procurements arrive in country as planned, Zambia will have full supply of ACTs. With FY 2016 funding, PMI will procure 3.3 million ACT treatments. In addition, PMI will provide support to increase prompt and effective treatment for uncomplicated malaria at the health facility level and support efforts to expand malaria treatment at the community level through integrated community case management (iCCM).

Pharmaceutical Management

In 2015 PMI provided support to the MOH/MCDMCH, MSL and other stakeholders to improve the collection, management, and use of logistics data through the roll-out of an electronic Logistics Management Information System (eLMIS). In 2015, MOH/MCDMCH, with support from partners, rolled out the eLMIS Central version to MSL, CHAZ, and all provincial and district eLMIS end users. In addition the redesigned EMLIP system was rolled out to 30 additional districts bringing the total trained districts to 68 districts (out of 106). It is estimated that rollout of the EMLIP hybrid system to the remaining districts will be completed by the end of June 2016. The Logistcs Management Unit at the MOH recorded a 98% reporting rate and improved commodity facility level stock availability (96%) for malaria commodities in EMLIP districts for the period January to June 2015 of FY 2015. In addition, according to monthly reports sent to the LMU from health facilities, the percentage of health facilities stocked out of all presentations of ACT fell from5% in June 2014 to 3% in April 2015. PMI continued to provide technical assistance at the national level through participation in working groups related to procurement and supply chain management. With FY 2016 funding, PMI will continue to support strengthening the GRZ's commodities supply and logistics systems at central, provincial, district, and health center level

Health systems strengthening and capacity building:

PMI supports a broad array of health system strengthening activities which cut across intervention areas, such as training of health workers, supply chain management and health information systems strengthening, drug efficacy monitoring, and NMCP capacity building. PMI has been providing technical assistance and capacity building at the NMCP including surveillance, monitoring and evaluation (SM&E) and community health worker training in iCCM. In addition, PMI used mapping technology, paired with health facility case data, to identify malaria hot spots within districts that were targeted for IRS. With FY 2016 funding, PMI will continue to support NMCP capacity building as well as support two Zambian nationals through the Field Epidemiology Training Program.

Behavior change communication (BCC):

The most recent NMCP BCC strategy ended in 2014. However, it continues to be in effect until a new strategy document is developed in 2015. The NMCP's BCC strategy for 2011–2014 has clear behavior change objectives for each of the malaria control interventions, and also identifies barriers to the desired behaviors. PMI supports an integrated community-based communications focusing on promotion of malaria prevention, diagnosis, appropriate treatment, and nutrition for pregnant women and children under five. In addition, PMI is supporting the MOH to strengthen malaria BCC by developing and implementing community-level BCC activities, which focus on malaria care seeking and prevention. With FY 2016 funding, PMI will support BCC implementation for malaria at both the national level and four target provinces (Luapula, Northern, Eastern, and Muchinga Provinces) at health facility and community levels to increase acceptance of IRS, increase ANC attendance with higher IPTp uptake, to improve healthcare-seeking behavior, and to increase demand for and acceptance of malaria diagnostics.

Monitoring and evaluation (M&E):

The revised Zambia NMSP 2011–2016 states that the objective of SM&E is to: "strengthen SM&E systems in order to ensure timely availability of quality, consistent and relevant data on malaria control performance by 2016." Along with the revised NMSP, a revised National M&E Plan will be developed to address the challenges in Zambia as it moves along malaria's epidemiological continuum. The national HMIS has been upgraded from the DHIS 1.4 to 2.0 nationwide. Malaria surveillance systems were developed for Southern Province at the facility level using the malaria rapid reporting system, mobile phones, and geographic information system. Health care workers report malaria cases, laboratory testing, and drug availability by web-enabled cell phones on a weekly basis. The previously PMI-supported enhanced surveillance in Lusaka District has been transitioned over to the Lusaka District Health Office. Active Infection Detection is ongoing in 23 of the 28 district health facilities. The end-use verification survey collects data on malaria commodities every month from facilities to assess availability. Monitoring and evaluating malaria prevention and control activities will rely on a combination of routine malaria data through the HMIS and surveys. With FY 2016 funds, PMI will provide support to strengthen routine malaria data collection at the community, health facility, district, and provincial levels through the HMIS. PMI will also support the next MIS. The NMCP is considering whether the next MIS will be in 2017 or 2018.

Operational research (OR):

The NMCP in Zambia has many ongoing and planned research activities with a number of different partners. In FY 2015, PMI supported the NMCP to develop an Operational Research Agenda to better map out current and future operational research activities and goals. This will be used to help coordinate current research activities and for planning purposes to align future research activities with the goals of the NMCP. PMI supported an operational research project on ITN durability that is currently ongoing. In addition, PMI is supporting a study to assess the associations between malaria control scale-up and micro-economic indicators in Zambia. Another study is looking at the impact and cost-effectiveness of focal IRS with pirimiphos-methyl in Nchelenge District. As of 2011, Zambia emphasizes universal coverage of ITNs with targeted IRS. Historically, vector control was split, with IRS reserved for urban and peri-urban areas while ITNs were targeted to rural areas. A proposed study would seek to shed light on how to determine where IRS would be best targeted in combination with universal ITN coverage. With FY 2016 funding, PMI will continue to support ongoing operations research activities around targeted IRS.

II. STRATEGY

1. Introduction

When it was launched in 2005, the goal of PMI was to reduce malaria-related mortality by 50% across 15 high-burden countries in sub-Saharan Africa through a rapid scale-up of four proven and highly effective malaria prevention and treatment measures: insecticide-treated mosquito nets (ITNs); indoor residual spraying (IRS); accurate diagnosis and prompt treatment with artemisinin-based combination therapies (ACTs); and intermittent preventive treatment for pregnant women (IPTp). With the passage of the Tom Lantos and Henry J. Hyde Global Leadership against HIV/AIDS, Tuberculosis, and Malaria Act in 2008, PMI developed a U.S. Government Malaria Strategy for 2009-2014. This strategy included a long-term vision for malaria control in which sustained high coverage with malaria prevention and treatment interventions would progressively lead to malaria-free zones in Africa, with the ultimate goal of worldwide malaria eradication by 2040-2050. Consistent with this strategy and the increase in annual appropriations supporting PMI, four new sub-Saharan African countries and one regional program in the Greater Mekong Subregion of Southeast Asia were added in 2011. The contributions of PMI, together with those of other partners, have led to dramatic improvements in the coverage of malaria control interventions in PMI-supported countries, and all 15 original countries have documented substantial declines in all-cause mortality rates among children less than five years of age.

In 2015, PMI launched the next six-year strategy, setting forth a bold and ambitious goal and objectives. The PMI Strategy for 2015-2020 takes into account the progress over the past decade and the new challenges that have arisen. Malaria prevention and control remains a major U.S. foreign assistance objective and PMI's Strategy fully aligns with the U.S. Government's vision of ending preventable child and maternal deaths and ending extreme poverty. It is also in line with the goals articulated in the draft RBM Partnership's second Global Malaria Action Plan and WHO's draft Global Technical Strategy. Under the PMI Strategy for 2015-2020, the U.S. Government's goal is to work with PMI-supported countries and partners to further reduce malaria deaths and substantially decrease malaria morbidity, towards the long-term goal of elimination.

Zambia was selected as a PMI focus country in FY 2007.

This Fiscal Year (FY) 2016 Malaria Operational Plan presents a detailed implementation plan for Zambia, based on the strategies of PMI and the National Malaria Control Program (NMCP) strategy. It was developed in consultation with the NMCP and with the participation of national and international partners involved in malaria prevention and control in the country. The activities that PMI is proposing to support fit in well with the National Malaria Control strategy and plan and build on investments made by PMI and other partners to improve and expand malaria-related services, including the Global Fund to Fight AIDS, Tuberculosis, and Malaria (Global Fund) malaria grants. This document briefly reviews the current status of malaria control policies and interventions in Zambia, describes progress to date, identifies challenges and unmet needs to achieving the targets of the NMCP and PMI, and provides a description of activities that are planned with FY 2016 funding.

2. Malaria situation in Zambia

Zambia has a 2015 estimated population of almost 15.5 million people (Central Statistics Office), with 40% residing in urban and 60% residing in rural areas. The country consists of 10 provinces and 106 districts (redistricting in 2015 increased the number of districts from 72 original districts). Recently, Zambia has made progress towards the Millennium Development Goals (MDG) targets for 2015. According to the 2014 Zambia Demographic and Health Survey (DHS), under-five mortality has fallen from 192 deaths per 1,000 live births in 1992 to 75 deaths per 1,000 live births in 2014. The literacy rate of 15 to 24 year olds stands at 81%. Lastly, Zambia has exceeded the MDG target for HIV/AIDS prevalence of 15.6% with 6.6% of the population age 15 to 24 living with HIV/AIDS (2014 DHS). Despite these positive trends, Zambia continues to face major challenges. There continues to be an economic divide between the urban and rural populations, with the proportion of population living in extreme poverty at 13.1% for urban and 57.7% for rural areas (MDG Progress Report, Zambia, 2013).

Malaria transmission in Zambia occurs year-round with peak transmission during the rainy season, between November and April. Malaria remains endemic but with wide variation in prevalence of infection across districts (2012 Malaria Indicator Survey (MIS)). In Zambia, malaria is caused by the four main *Plasmodium* species that infect humans, with *Plasmodium falciparum* accounting for 98% of all infections. *Anopheles (An.) gambiae* and *An. funestus* are the major vectors. All ten provinces of Zambia are endemic for malaria with 90% of the population at risk. The NMCP first classified the country into three malaria epidemiological zones (Figure 1) to better focus their efforts after the 2010 MIS. This classification was updated following the 2012 MIS with North-Western Province dropping from Zone 2 to Zone 3.

- Zone 1: Areas where malaria control has markedly reduced transmission and parasite prevalence in children less than five years of age is less than 1% (Lusaka city and environs).
- Zone 2: Areas where sustained malaria prevention and control has markedly reduced transmission and parasite prevalence is at or under 14% in children under five years of age at the peak of transmission (Central, Copperbelt, Southern, and Western Provinces).
- Zone 3: Areas where progress in malaria control has been achieved but not sustained and lapses in prevention coverage have led to resurgence of infection and illness, and parasite prevalence in young children exceeds 14% at the peak of the transmission season (Eastern, Luapula, Muchinga, Northern, and North-Western Provinces).

Figure 1: National Malaria Control Program country classification of malaria epidemiological zones, 2013.

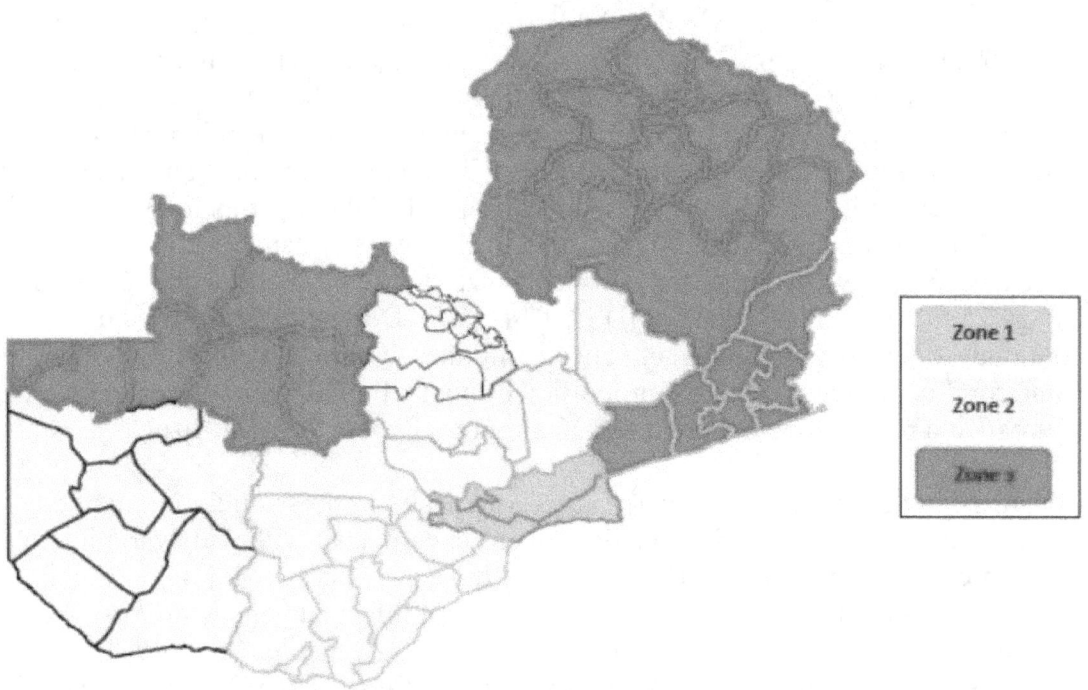

Overall, the number of reported malaria cases (clinical and confirmed) to the National Health Management Information System (HMIS) increased from 4,297,157 to 5,807,034 (2010-2014). However, it is important to note that HMIS reporting rates average about 65%. Further, Zambia has a large cadre of active community health workers that provide treatment for malaria at community level particularly in the rural areas. The treatment data from CHW is generally not reported in the national HMIS. A 2014 PMI-supported review showed that data challenges were the main reasons for the mismatch between reported cases in HMIS and antimalarial and RDT consumption data. Therefore, the real annual malaria burden is higher than that reported in the HMIS. The MOH, MCDMCH, and partners including PMI are making efforts to strengthen HMIS reporting.

The reported number of outpatient department (OPD) visits increased from 13,697,003 in 2009 to 21,668,763 in 2012. Between 2010 and 2014 substantial declines were recorded with reported inpatient malaria deaths for all ages decreasing from 3.9 per 1,000 to 2.4 per 1,000. Malaria parasite prevalence by smear microscopy has declined from 22% in 2006 to 15% in 2012, but has remained relatively unchanged during the period of 2010 – 2012 (16% - 15%) (Table A). Severe anemia for children under the age of five years also declined from 14% in 2006 to 7% in 2012. This was most notable in the provinces that reported higher ITN coverage compared to 2010, and in the higher prevalence area of Luapula Province. It is important to note that these national-level numbers are not representative of all the trends across the country and there are documented variations between provinces and districts. For instance, the largest relative decline in parasite prevalence by microscopy was observed in Luapula Province (51% - 32%) compared to 2010. North-Western Province had the largest relative increase in parasite prevalence (6% - 17%), while Northern Province remained relatively unchanged (24%).

Table A: Malaria parasite prevalence in children under five years of age by background characteristic from Malaria Indicator Surveys (MIS). Rapid Diagnostic Test (RDT) results in parenthesis, 2006-2012.

Background characteristic	Percentage with malaria parasites read by microscopy	Percentage with malaria parasites read by microscopy	Percentage with malaria parasites read by microscopy (or RDT)	Percentage with malaria parasites read by microscopy (or RDT)
	2006	2008	2010	2012
Age (in months)				
<12	12.6	3.6	5.7 (12.5)	9.8 (15.9)
12–23	22.8	10.2	12.1 (21.9)	11.7 (24.4)
24–35	25.3	11.2	20.1 (30.8)	16.3 (31.7)
36–47	26.3	13.8	21.4 (36.1)	16.2 (35.0)
48–59	24.4	12.5	22.0 (33.7)	19.6 (38.0)
Sex				
Male	21.9	10.5	16.9 (26.8)	14.7 (29.1)
Female	21.8	9.8	15.1 (26.7)	15.1 (30.0)
Residence				
Urban	6.4	4.3	5.2 (12.0)	3.7 (8.2)
Rural	27.8	12.4	20.4 (32.7)	20.2 (39.7)
Province				
Central	27.7	7.9	9.4 (11.5)	8.5 (12.8)
Copperbelt	12.4	9.9	12.1 (24.0)	4.7 (17.4)
Eastern	21.0	9.3	22.0 (50.1)	25.3 (51.1)
Luapula	32.9	21.8	50.5 (63.4)	32.1 (56.0)
Lusaka	0.8	1.7	0.0 (1.4)	0.0 (4.8)
Muchinga				19.4 (33.5)
Northern	35.3	12.0	23.6 (32.6)	23.7 (47.3)
North-Western	24.3	15.2	6.1 (17.3)	16.9 (32.5)
Southern	13.7	7.9	5.7 (12.2)	8.4 (10.0)
Western	11.1	2.6	5.1 (11.8)	12.6 (34.3)
Wealth index				
Lowest	30.4	13.1	29.2 (42.1)	27.4 (49.5)
Second	27.6	13.6	21.8 (36.2)	21.1 (42.8)
Middle	23.4	12.1	12.1 (22.9)	17.9 (35.1)
Fourth	7.5	6.7	9.4 (20.6)	13.9 (27.7)
Highest	6.2	2.8	1.4 (4.4)	1.8 (5.8)
Total	22.1	10.2	16.0 (26.7)	14.9 (29.5)

In addition, there has been an increase in the number of reported confirmed and clinical cases and deaths in North-Western Province. The HMIS also shows a trend in this geographic area of increasing malaria incidence during the period of 2011-2014. In Central Province malaria cases (reported confirmed and clinical) have increased significantly since 2011 and should be monitored to ensure that there is not a reversal of the progress that has been made in this area during the preceding years. Reported malaria inpatients and deaths have declined over the past five years and this could be due in part to improved case management at the health facility level. The following table (Table B) shows HMIS reporting of cases (clinical and confirmed), inpatients, and deaths during the period of 2010-2014.

Table B: Health Management Information Systems (HMIS) reported cases, deaths and inpatients, 2010-2014. Reporting rate as of 2014 at 65%					
Period	**2010**	**2011**	**2012**	**2013**	**2014**
Cases (clinical and confirmed)					
HMIS malaria cases total clinical	2,967,065	2,207,992	2,063,921	2,345,972	1,945,490
HMIS malaria cases total confirmed	1,330,092	2,227,904	2,696,983	2,546,841	3,861,544
HMIS malaria cases total	4,297,157	4,435,896	4,760,904	4,892,813	5,807,034
Inpatient cases and deaths					
HMIS malaria inpatient cases total	185,488	174,040	158,001	160,010	135,732
HMIS malaria deaths	5,133	4,357	3,898	3,841	2,974
Inpatient cases and deaths (<5yr)					
HMIS malaria inpatient cases total, <5yr	107,068	99,067	86,385	86,727	64,786
HMIS malaria deaths, <5yrs	2,949	2,580	2,248	2,390	1,654

Figure 2: Health Management Information System (HMIS) reported malaria incidence (per 1,000) by district during 2014.

3. Country health system delivery structure and Ministry of Health organization

Following the change of government in October 2011, the Zambian Government re-aligned the health portfolio functions between the Ministry of Health (MOH) and the Ministry of Community Development Mother and Child Health (MCDMCH). Under the new arrangement, the Ministry of Health is responsible for planning, health policy guidelines, surveillance, monitoring and evaluation, allocating funds, and sourcing key health inputs including drugs and equipment for service delivery. The MCDMCH is responsible for providing technical oversight for the implementation of health activities at district, health center, health post, and community levels.

Figure 3: Health Structure and Organization

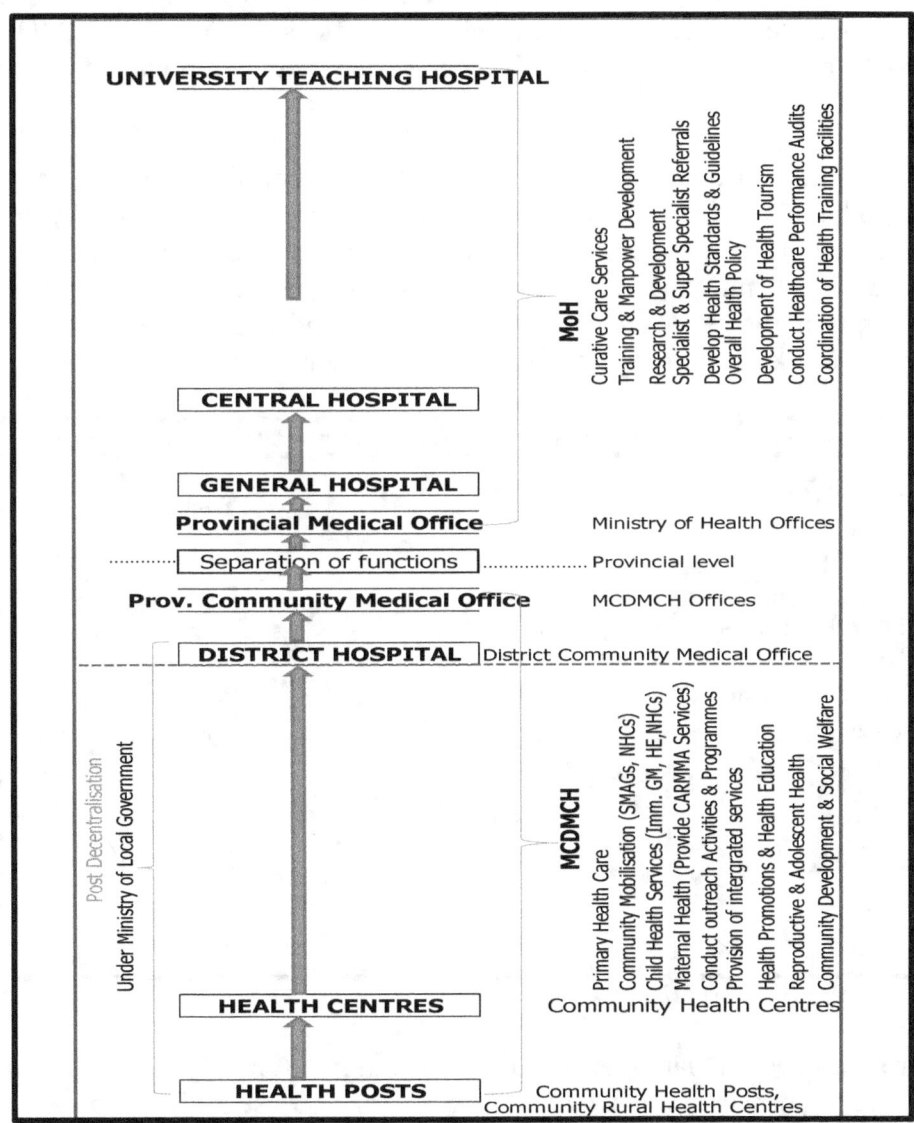

Government-run health facilities, which provide the majority of the health care in Zambia, offer a basic health care package of high-impact interventions. Services included in the basic health care package are provided free-of-charge or on a cost-sharing basis, depending on the location and level of the system. In rural districts these services are free. The following are the levels of health care facilities offered throughout the country (Figure 3); malaria control interventions are delivered in all of them.

- Community
- Health posts (district level)
- Health centers (district level)
- Level 1 hospitals (district level), Level 2 hospitals (provincial level), and Level 3 hospitals (central level)

Activities such as implementation of IRS, ITN distribution, and malaria case management at level 1 hospitals, health centers, and community levels are the responsibility of MCDMCH implemented through the District Community Medical Offices (DCMOs). The MOH/National Malaria Control Centre (NMCC) will provide technical but not operational assistance at these levels.

Provincial Health Offices are supervised by the MOH. However, they have reporting responsibilities to both the MOH and MCDMCH. DCMOs are commissioned by the MCDMCH to provide services at the district and community level. The second- and third-level hospitals are referral or specialized hospitals. Due to resource constraints, however, there is generally a variation between what the levels are supposed to provide and what they actually do provide. Table C shows the breakdown by type of facility and provider.

Table C: Summary of health facilities by type and provider, Zambia, 2012		
Facility Type	Total	Percentage of Facilities
Health Posts	307	16
Rural Health Centers	1,131	58
Urban Health Centers	409	21
Level 1 Hospitals	84	4
Level 2 Hospitals	19	<1
Level 3 Hospitals	6	<1
Total	1,956	100
Health Facilities By Provider		
MOH	1,590	81
Mission	116	6
Private	250	13
Total	1,956	100

Source: Ministry of Health, 2012

The DCMO provides overall planning, coordination, and monitoring of malaria activities within their districts. Health posts are intended to cover 500–1,000 households. A newly created cadre of community health assistants (CHAs), trained for one year and part of the government pay role, has been deployed at some health posts in selected districts. At the community level, community health workers (CHWs) provide malaria diagnostic and treatment services through the integrated community case management (iCCM) program. Health centers, staffed by a clinical officer, nurse, or environmental health technician, serve a catchment area of approximately 10,000 residents. In 2010, it was estimated that in urban areas, approximately 99% of households are within five kilometers of a health facility, compared to 50% in rural areas. In 2012, Lusaka Province had the highest number of health facilities (294) followed by Southern (253), and the Copperbelt Province (250). Muchinga, the newly created province, had the lowest number of health facilities (99).

In addition to the MOH, the Churches Health Association of Zambia (CHAZ), parastatal organizations, private clinics, and traditional healers also provide health care in Zambia. CHAZ is an inter-denominational umbrella organization for coordinating church health services in Zambia that has 116 health facilities (Table C) including hospitals, health centers, health posts, and community-based organizations, and 11 health training schools, most of which are staffed by Government of Zambia health workers. Altogether, these institutions are responsible for over 50% of formal health services in the rural areas of Zambia and about 30% of health care in the country as a whole.

There over 250 for-profit private health facilities (Table C) in Zambia, most of which are clinics attending to outpatients only, and are located mainly in the urban districts. In addition, private mining companies provide preventive and curative medical services for their workers and families, as well as surrounding communities in some cases. Several of the larger mining companies, such as Konkola and Mopani Copper Mines, have been carrying out IRS for a number of years within and around their compounds.

4. National malaria control strategy

The 2011-2015 National Malaria Strategic Plan (NMSP) underwent a midterm review in 2013. As a result of the review, the NMSP was extended by an additional year to run through 2016. The vision of the revised NMSP is to achieve progress towards a "malaria-free Zambia" through equity of access to quality-assured, cost-effective malaria prevention and control interventions close to the household. The NMSP aims to achieve the following three goals by 2016: 1) reduce malaria incidence by 75% from the 2010 baseline; 2) reduce malaria deaths to near zero and reduce all-cause child mortality by 20%; and 3) establish and maintain five "malaria-free zones" in Zambia.

The following overall changes were made to the NMSP following the 2013 mid-term review:
- A clear statement that the MCDMCH is now part of the NMCP,
- Emphasis on achieving and maintaining universal ITN coverage while utilizing a focal data driven approach to prioritize IRS,
- Greater attention paid to the coordination, leadership, governance, and resource mobilization role of the NMCP for effective and efficient management, and
- Emphasis on iCCM rather than community management of malaria.

The NMCP aims to strengthen national-, provincial-, and district-level capacity to plan, manage, and implement malaria activities; address human resource needs; ensure that there is an established planning and forecasting framework for projecting funding needs and tracking health expenditures; develop capacity at all levels of the health system to manage the storage and distribution of malaria commodities; and reinforce coordination among partners. The plan seeks to have 100% of households and persons at risk in targeted areas have access to evidence-based vector control and other preventive interventions by 2016. The NMCP will aim to achieve and sustain universal ITN coverage and utilize a focal data-driven approach to prioritize IRS. The plan also seeks to improve malaria case management, diagnostic testing capacity and quality as well as increase coverage of three doses of sulfadoxine-pyrimethamine (SP) for IPTp. In addition, the plan notes the need to strengthen behavior change communication (BCC) for malaria prevention and treatment, and the importance of establishing a robust surveillance, and monitoring and evaluation (SM&E) framework.

5. Updates in the strategy section

The NMCP released a synopsis of the follow-on to the current NMSP 2011-2016 in April 2015. The main two goals of the new strategic plan "Moving from accelerated burden reduction to malaria elimination: the Zambia 2015–2020 strategy" are to eliminate local malaria infection within Zambia's boundaries by 2020, and to maintain malaria-free status and prevent reintroduction due to importation of malaria in areas where the disease has been eliminated. The strategy includes annual milestones for each year leading to malaria elimination by 2020. To support this new strategy, and in addition to the technical interventions (ITNs, IRS, MIP, CM, HSS, SM&E, OR, and BCC) described in the NMSP 2011-2016, the NMCP is considering including mass drug administration (MDA) with dihydroartemisinin-piperaquine (DHA-PQ) among the interventions in the elimination strategy. The NMCP plans to conduct an evaluation of the malaria program in 2016 that will include costing of the elimination strategy.

Starting in 2015, the Global Fund will provide funds to support the Trans-Zambezi Malaria Initiative that aims to eliminate malaria in the Zambezi valley covering Zambia and Zimbabwe. The initiative aims to accelerate reduction of malaria transmission among border communities through implementation of coordinated malaria control activities.

6. Integration, collaboration, and coordination

The NMCP and its collaborating partners maintain regular communications and coordinate efforts through routine partners' meetings and technical working groups on IRS, BCC, SM&E, case management, ITNs, and operational research. All partners contributed to the development of the new 2011-2015 National Malaria Strategic Plan (NMSP), annual action plans, and the 2015-2017 Global Fund Concept Note.

In FY 2014, a universal campaign was conducted that distributed over 8 million ITNs nationwide. The campaign was a collaborative effort between the NMCP, PMI, DFID, Global Fund, MACEPA and other partners. PMI contributed approximately 1 million ITNs for the campaign. PMI also partnered with PEPFAR to purchase 600,000 ITNs for counseling and testing sites in high prevalence areas for malaria. In 2015 and 2016, PMI will collaborate with Peace Corps to conduct net durability monitoring in Northern and Luapula provinces. Twenty

Peace Corps volunteers (PCVs) living in these two provinces will assist with data collection for the activity. PMI has assisted with the revision of the GRZ Malaria Diagnostic and Treatment Guidelines that was based upon World Health Organization (WHO) Guidelines.

PMI meets regularly with the WHO, United Nations Development Program (UNDP), United Nations Children's Fund (UNICEF), MOH, Global Fund, Akros, MACEPA, Clinton Health Access Initiative (CHAI), Isdell Flowers Foundation, and Bill and Melinda Gates Foundation staff to ensure coordination of efforts and utilization of lessons learned from the various partners to improve implementation of malaria interventions.

Table D provides a breakdown of the projected financial contributions of the different organizations to the malaria program over the course of the years 2015–2017.

Table D: Malaria Financial Contribution (2015-17)				
Funding Source	2015	2016	2017	TOTAL
GRZ	28,000,000	28,500,000	29,000,000	85,500,000
Global Fund[2]	18,876,269	19,271,102	43,476,805	81,624,176
PMI	24,000,000	24,000,000	24,000,000	72,000,000
DFID	7,200,000	0	0	7,200,000
WHO & UNICEF	300,000	300,000	300,000	900,000
MACEPA	2,500,000	0	0	2,500,000
PRIVATE SECTOR	1,124,832	1,181,074	1,240,128	3,546,034
TOTAL FUNDING	82,001,101	73,252,176	98,016,933	253,270,210

Sources:
1. *Global Fund Concept Note Application (2015-17)*
2. *Global Fund Grant Performance Report Zambia (MOH and CHAZ) – 19 February 2015)*

7. PMI goal, objectives, strategic areas, and key indicators

Under the PMI Strategy for 2015 - 2020, the U.S. Government's goal is to work with PMI-supported countries and partners to further reduce malaria deaths and substantially decrease malaria morbidity, towards the long-term goal of elimination. Building upon the progress to date in PMI-supported countries, PMI will work with NMCPs and partners to accomplish the following objectives by 2020:

1. Reduce malaria mortality by one-third from 2015 levels in PMI-supported countries, achieving a greater than 80% reduction from PMI's original 2000 baseline levels.

2. Reduce malaria morbidity in PMI-supported countries by 40% from 2015 levels.

3. Assist at least five PMI-supported countries to meet the WHO criteria for national or sub-national pre-elimination.[1]

---

[1] http://whqlibdoc.who.int/publications/2007/9789241596084_eng.pdf

These objectives will be accomplished by emphasizing five core areas of strategic focus:

1. Achieving and sustaining scale of proven interventions
2. Adapting to changing epidemiology and incorporating new tools
3. Improving countries' capacity to collect and use information
4. Mitigating risk against the current malaria control gains
5. Building capacity and health systems towards full country ownership

To track progress toward achieving and sustaining scale of proven interventions (area of strategic focus #1), PMI will continue to track the key indicators recommended by the Roll Back Malaria Monitoring and Evaluation Reference Group (RBM MERG) as listed below:

- Proportion of households with at least one ITN
- Proportion of households with at least one ITN for every two people
- Proportion of children under five years old who slept under an ITN the previous night
- Proportion of pregnant women who slept under an ITN the previous night
- Proportion of households in targeted districts protected by IRS
- Proportion of children under five years old with fever in the last two weeks for whom advice or treatment was sought
- Proportion of children under five with fever in the last two weeks who had a finger or heel stick
- Proportion receiving an ACT among children under five years old with fever in the last two weeks who received any antimalarial drugs
- Proportion of women who received two or more doses of IPTp for malaria during ANC visits during their last pregnancy

8. Progress on coverage/impact indicators to date

At the national level, the 2014 DHS showed encouraging malaria prevention and control coverage. Key findings are as follows:

- 73% of households have at least one mosquito net; 68% have at least one ITN, the majority of which are long-lasting insecticidal nets.
- 28% of households reported that they had received IRS during the past 12 months.
- On the night before the survey, 41% of children under age five slept under an ITN. Among households with at least one ITN, 57% of children under age five slept under an ITN.
- Overall, 41% of pregnant women slept under an ITN the night before the survey. Among pregnant women living in households that possess an ITN, 62% slept under an ITN the night before the survey.
- 73% of women who had their last birth in the two years preceding the survey received IPTp during their pregnancy; women taking two or more doses of SP and received at least one of those doses during an ANC visit.
- 91% of children with a fever in the two weeks preceding the survey who took antimalarial drugs were treated with an ACT.

Since the 2014 DHS did not collect parasitemia, the most recent national parasitemia is from the 2012 MIS. The 2012 MIS demonstrated a steady increase in intervention coverage and a continued reduction in the malaria parasite prevalence since 2006: 15% of children ages 0–59 months had malaria parasitemia (microscopy) in 2012, compared to 16% in 2010 and 22% in 2006 (Table E).

Table E: Evolution of Key Malaria Indicators in Zambia from 2006 to 2014

Indicator	2006 MIS[1]	2008 MIS[2]	2010 MIS[3]	2012 MIS[4]	2014 DHS[5]
% Households with at least one ITN	38	62	64	68	73
% Households with at least one ITN per sleeping space	NA	33	34	55	27
% Children under five who slept under an ITN the previous night	24	41	50	57	41
% Pregnant women who slept under an ITN the previous night	25	43	46	58	41
% Households in targeted districts protected by IRS	26	43	23	25	28
% Children under five years old with fever in the last two weeks for whom advice or treatment was sought	60	64	31	25	75
% Children under five with fever in the last two weeks who had a finger or heel stick	NA	11	17	32	49
% Children receiving an ACT among children under five years old with fever in the last two weeks who received any antimalarial drugs	18	30	76	85	91
% Women who received two or more doses of IPTp during their last pregnancy in the last two years	59	66	70	72	73

1. Zambia Ministry of Health, 2006. Zambia National Malaria Indicator Survey 2006. Lusaka, Zambia: Ministry of Health.
2. Zambia Ministry of Health, 2008. Zambia National Malaria Indicator Survey 2008. Lusaka, Zambia: Ministry of Health.
3. Zambia Ministry of Health, 2010. Zambia National Malaria Indicator Survey 2010. Lusaka, Zambia: Ministry of Health.
4. Zambia Ministry of Health, 2012. Zambia National Malaria Indicator Survey 2012. Lusaka, Zambia: Ministry of Health.
5. Zambia Ministry of Health, 2014. Zambia Demographic Health Survey 2014, Lusaka, Zambia: Ministry of Health.

However, progress is not homogeneous throughout the country. Household ownership of at least one ITN ranges from 90% in Luapula Province to 52% in Western Province, and the percentage of households with at least one ITN per sleeping space varied from 83% in Luapula Province to 38% in Lusaka Province. Luapula Province's high ITN coverage likely contributed to a large drop in parasite prevalence. Lusaka Province parasite prevalence continues to remain very low and the prevalence in the Copperbelt Province improved, although HMIS data (malaria incidence rate of 402 per 1,000 in 2013) is not consistent with a parasite prevalence of 4% (Figure 4). Malaria prevalence decreased between 2006 and 2008 in four provinces (Southern, Central, Muchinga, and Northern), but has since remained stable. Parasite prevalence in Eastern Province has not changed from 2006 to 2012. Finally, parasite prevalence in two provinces (Western and North-Western) increased in 2012 after significant declines between 2006 and 2010 (Figure 4).

Figure 4: MIS reported malaria parasite prevalence (microscopy) among children under five years of age

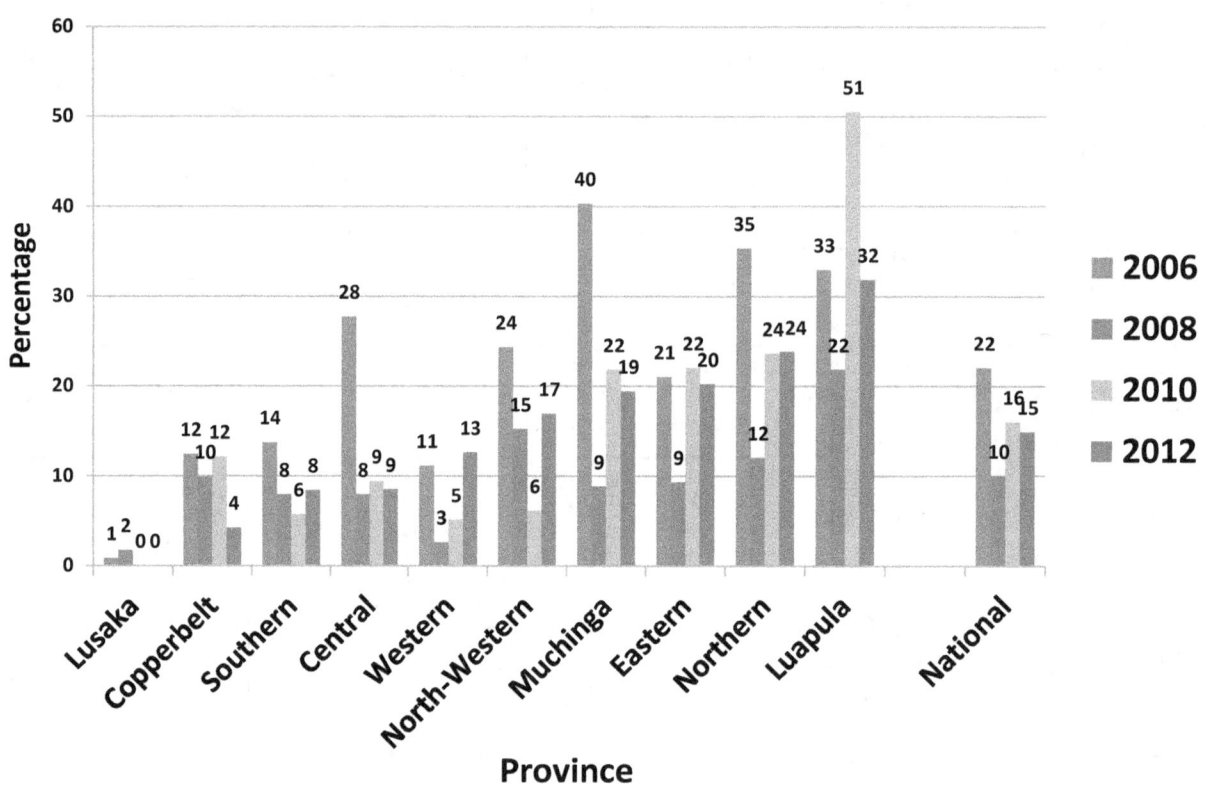

9. Other relevant evidence on progress

The last nationwide health facility survey was in 2011. It provides insight into the preparedness of health facilities to deliver quality malaria services. The survey included 148 health facilities, of which 41 were hospitals, 38 were urban health centers, 39 were rural health centers and 30 were health posts. A total of 219 health workers were observed and 1,290 patients were assessed, of which 872 were suspected of having malaria. Key findings are:

- Testing for malaria was generally available; highest in hospitals (93%) and lowest in health posts (63%).
- The first-line drug also was available; most frequently in hospitals (95%) than in health posts (73%)

- Approximately one-third of health workers had not received an in-service training in the last five years.
- Testing of suspected malaria reached 76% in children under five years of age.
- Seventy-three percent of "true positives" (after re-examination) received appropriate antimalarial treatment.

A program of enhanced surveillance and active community case detection and laboratory confirmation in Lusaka District has shown low levels of transmission. In 2011–2012, 395 index cases (17% of all cases of confirmed malaria) that had not traveled or had malaria in the month prior to testing were identified. A total of 5,795 persons associated with the index cases were tested in their homes or nearby homes. Only 91 (1.6%) of these neighborhood members were positive by RDT. The success of this program has been evident in the decision of the district health officials to take over funding in all 29 clinics in Lusaka District. This surveillance activity has also been implemented in selected clinics in seven other districts in Southern Province to help document elimination of malaria in five districts in Zambia by 2015.

10. Challenges and opportunities

Important challenges for PMI continue to be the re-organization of the malaria control activities under the MOH and the MCDMCH and the availability of funds to carry out activities at the district and community levels. During this MOP planning visit, PMI planned jointly with both the MOH and MCDMCH. MCDMCH has recruited and filled a number of key positions at the central level. However, availability of operational funds for the recruited staff to perform their respective tasks such as regular supportive supervision to the districts remains a major challenge. The MCDMCH continues to work with MOH and other stakeholders to ensure that funding for primary health functions previously under MOH are reflected in the MCDMCH budget, although considerable improvement has been made in this regard. PMI's Resident Advisors will follow the re-structuring process closely to ensure that there are no disruptions in PMI activities.

An important challenge for malaria control in Zambia, especially in an environment in which donor funds are stabilizing and even decreasing globally, is the heavy dependence on external funding. The shift of DIFD resources away from malaria control activities in Zambia, for example, will leave a major gap in FY 2016 and beyond. DFID has been an important partner in procurement of ITN, RDTs, ACTs, and essential medicines as well as supporting IRS in Luapula and Central provinces. PMI, DFID, the Global fund, and several other partners have been instrumental in working with the GRZ to increase governmental funding for malaria. Capital and revolving costs have been mainly borne by donor partners since 2004. The MOH recognizes this dependence problem and has begun to increase its own funding for malaria control. The MOH procures all SP for IPTp and has included $20 million in its current budget (to be applied during 2015) to support several malaria activities.

Zambia is moving into a new era of malaria control in which approaches and tools that have served well thus far to reach the current coverage levels will need to be revised to address the challenges of reaching the last mile. From dealing with late adopters of appropriate malaria behaviors to ensuring that commodities get to those hardest to reach, to developing monitoring and evaluation methods that provide accurate estimates in low prevalence settings, Zambia will need to maintain its gains while dealing with new scenarios to gain additional ground.

III. OPERATIONAL PLAN

PMI fully supports all elements of the NMCP's national malaria strategy. The vision of the revised NMSP is to achieve progress towards a "malaria-free Zambia" through equity of access to quality-assured, cost-effective malaria prevention and control interventions close to the household. PMI will continue to provide technical support to the NMCP at central level, procure malaria commodities including anti-malarial drugs and ITNs for country-wide distribution and support improved laboratory diagnosis and clinical management of malaria nationally. However, beginning 2015, PMI will focus province and district level efforts in four high malaria burden provinces (36 districts). The decision was based on the following: (1) Data indicate that four provinces are lagging behind the national trend and will lessen further advances in national coverage indicators if no additional support is provided; (2) Population in the four provinces is significant—5 million people, or one third of the population of the country—and suffer a disproportionate one half of all malaria burden; (3) PMI resources cannot address all national operational needs and therefore must be used judiciously if PMI and national malaria control objectives are to be reached; (4) PMI is the best placed donor, both technically and administratively, to focus attention on the disadvantaged provinces. This shift in PMI strategy was requested by the NMCP and discussed with other donors to ensure that needs in other provinces are addressed. PMI's malaria control efforts will continue to focus on high burden provinces.

In addition to the NMSP, PMI has been involved in the development of the elimination strategy. Implementation of this strategy still needs to be defined and PMI will work with NMCP and others to estimate costs and identify activities to move towards elimination. At this time, the role of PMI is still to be determined.

1. Insecticide-treated nets

NMCP/PMI objectives

Zambia's Strategic Plan calls for universal net coverage, which is defined as "ensuring all sleeping spaces in targeted households are covered by an ITN." The revised NMSP (2011–2016) makes universal ITN coverage the main strategy for achieving sustained vector control for all people at risk of malaria infection in the country. IRS will be added to ITNs in densely populated areas with insecticide resistance and high malaria burden.

In order to achieve universal coverage, a number of delivery methods have been adopted. These include free mass distribution of ITNs and routine distribution to pregnant women and children under-five years of age through ANC and EPI clinics. Further, in 2015, the NMCP plans to roll-out community-based distribution, as well as school-based distribution to enhance routine distribution efforts.

Progress since PMI was launched

As a result of various distribution efforts, the percentage of homes with at least one ITN increased from 38% in 2006 to 68% in 2012.[2] The percentage of household members that slept under an ITN increased from 19% in 2006 to 49% in 2012.[3] Despite the progress, ITN coverage remains below the country's universal coverage target prior to 2015. In addition, the 2012 MIS showed that ITN coverage also varies across provinces, ranging from 52% in Western, to 90% in Luapula. To address falling coverage levels in some provinces, the NMCP conducted a national mass ITN campaign for 2013-2014. The GRZ received financial and technical support for the mass campaign from a number of stakeholders, including PMI, the Global Fund, DFID, UNICEF, WHO, MACEPA, and others.

The NMCP has a target of 80% use of ITNs by children under five years and pregnant women by 2016. ITN use in children under five increased from 24% in 2006 to 57% in 2012.[4] Eastern Province reported the highest under-five use at 80% and Lusaka had the lowest at 40%. The under-five utilization was 68% nationally in households with at least one ITN. Fifty-eight percent of pregnant women reported sleeping under an ITN in 2012, ranging from 39% in Copperbelt to 89% in Eastern.

Progress during the last 12-18 months

To achieve the goal for universal net coverage, a rolling mass distribution campaign was conducted during a period of 18 months to distribute over 8 million ITNs nationwide. The mass distribution campaign was a collaborative effort between the NMCP, PMI, Global Fund, DFID, UNDP, MACEPA, and other partners. The campaign started in Western Province in FY 2014 with support from DFID and PMI as a door-to-door campaign that distributed 770,000 ITNs to cover every sleeping space. Copperbelt Province also conducted a mass campaign in FY 2014 with support from the World Bank and PMI. PMI contributed 652,000 ITNs to the campaign in Copperbelt. Mass campaigns also occurred in rural districts of Lusaka Province during the first quarter of FY 2014 as well as in selected districts in Eastern Province.

In FY 2015, mass campaigns occurred in Eastern, Central, Northwestern, Southern, Muchinga, Northern, and Luapula Provinces. PMI partnered with World Vision in Luapula Province. PMI provided enough ITNs to assure universal coverage in Luapula, while World Vision provided private donor funding to support distribution costs. Global Fund/UNDP supported the remaining six provinces. The GRZ plans to implement its next universal coverage campaign in 2017.

Following the campaign, which was in most part a success, a number of key challenges have been identified. Quantifications for ITN needs were based on census data from the Central Statistics office. Preliminary reports show that the census-based calculations underestimated the actual need. All provinces except Luapula have reported gaps in universal coverage goals. The extent of these gaps is still being determined by reconciling the number of nets that were distributed to the number of bed spaces that were registered just prior to distribution. Campaign

---

[2] Malaria Indicator Survey 2006, 2012
[3] Malaria Indicator Survey 2006, 2012
[4] Malaria Indicator Survey 2006, 2012

distribution efforts varied across provinces with some provinces distributing ITNs door-to-door, while other provinces distributed ITNs from central distribution points. Anecdotally, areas that used the door-to-door approach achieved better coverage than areas that distributed through central distribution points. This discrepancy is yet to be validated. In addition to determining the ITN gap in distribution, efforts are underway to determine net utilization following the mass campaign distribution, to ensure that those who have access to an ITN are using it correctly and consistently. Net misuse has also been identified as a potential challenge in a number of fishing communities. There have been anecdotal reports of the use of ITNs for fishing, which are being investigated to determine the extent of the misuse, which as of writing this MOP remains unquantified.

PMI supports continuous ITN distribution to vulnerable populations in Zambia by providing ITNs for distribution at ANC and EPI clinics. PMI also partnered with PEPFAR to purchase 600,000 ITNs for counseling and testing sites in high prevalence areas for malaria. PMI is also supporting the expansion from facility-based distribution channels to include school-based and community-based distribution. In January 2014, PMI supported a situational analysis as well as national and provincial level continuous distribution workshops with key stakeholders. The analysis concluded that ANC and EPI facility-based channels were not sufficient to replace worn out nets over time, and additional channels were required. After reviewing different scenarios, a consensus was reached to add primary schools and community-based distributions to the existing ANC and EPI channels. Modelling estimations showed that these four channels can maintain ITN ownership levels at 90%. PMI supported the development of a draft Zambia Continuous/Routine Distribution Guideline.

In 2015, a school-based distribution pilot will begin in four provinces: Luapula, Northern, Eastern, and Muchinga. Each province will receive an orientation for school-based distribution and a national committee will be established to oversee district and provincial training for school based distribution. In July 2015, initial pilot activities began in four districts in Luapula Province, targeting students in grade one and grade three to receive new ITNs in coordination with National School Health and Nutrition Month.

In 2015, community-based distribution activities will be based on a voucher program. Districts will be supplied with six months stock of ITNs required for community distribution, while health centers will be supplied with three months of stock. In each pilot district, selected health centers will identify an ITN voucher distributor that will cover an identified catchment area. The ITN voucher distributor will be provided with coupons and will verify need in the community, in collaboration with other community based groups (e.g., village health committees, Safe Motherhood Action Groups (SMAGs), etc.). Community members will be provided with a coupon that they can turn in for a new ITN at their respective health center.

PMI supported an operational research study aimed at describing attrition, physical integrity, and insecticide persistence of ITNs over time to better estimate net lifespan. ITNs distributed in 2011 in Northern and Luapula Provinces were being tracked and examined for structural integrity and insecticide content through December 2013. Data was collected by Peace Corps volunteers at the provincial and local levels. PMI is also supporting net durability monitoring of nets that were distributed during the FY 2014/FY 2015 campaign. Similar to previous net durability monitoring efforts, data will be collected by Peace Corps Volunteers at the provincial and local levels.

Commodity gap analysis

Table F. ITN Gap Analysis

Calendar Year	2015	2016	2017
Total Targeted Population	15,031,200	15,452,074	15,884,732
Continuous Distribution Needs			
Channel #1: ANC	781,622	803,508	826,007
Channel #2: EPI	73,851	75,541	77,656
Channel #3: Community		TBD*	TBD*
Channel #4: School		TBD*	TBD*
Estimated Total Need for Continuous	855,473	879,049	903,663
Mass Distribution Needs			
Mass distribution campaign	7,699,269		8,132,961
Estimated Total Need for Campaigns	7,699,269	0	8,132,961
Total Calculated Need: Routine and Campaign	**8,554,742**	**879,049**	**9,036,624**
Partner Contributions			
ITNs carried over from previous year	7,337,533	0	1,128,436
ITNs from MOH	200,000	0	0
ITNs from Global Fund Round	0	857,436	3,289,316
ITNs from Other Donors	0	800,000	0
ITNs planned with PMI funding	800,000	350,000	900,000
Total ITNs Available	**8,337,533**	**2,007,436**	**5,317,752**
Total ITN Surplus (Gap)	**(217,209)**	**1,128,436**	**(3,718,872)**

Notes: The ITN population-based gap analysis is based on the official population figures for Zambia, minus the estimated Lusaka urban population (Total ITN need per year does not include Lusaka Urban).

To reach one ITN per two people, ITN quantification is calculated based on an estimate of one ITN per 1.8 persons, plus 10% to account for inaccuracies in population projections.

*At the writing of this MOP, the quantification of ITNs for school-based and community-based distribution have not yet been finalized. The annual net requirements are expected to be modest and will not significantly affect quantifications for other distribution channels.

Plans and justification

With FY 2016 funding, PMI will focus on the procurement and distribution of ITNs for the 2017 mass distribution campaign. The most recent mass distribution campaign was conducted on a rolling basis over a period of 18 months. Distributions began in December of 2013 and continued through June of 2015. The next campaign, which would begin in 2017 and go through 2018, would be staggered in a similar manner. In addition, the distribution schedule for the 2017/2018 campaign would be determined by the distribution schedule that was followed in 2013-2015. In other words, areas that received nets in December 2013 would be the first to receive nets in the next campaign. Areas that received nets last, in June of 2015 would be the last to receive nets in 2018. This would mean that the period between mass distributions would be 36 months or more. PMI will continue to provide technical assistance for the roll out of primary school and community distribution. In addition, PMI will continue to monitor the durability of ITNs distributed during the 2013/2014 mass campaign. In order to maximize ITN usage, PMI will continue to support BCC activities, prioritizing local over national activities.

Proposed activities with FY 2016 funding: ($3,863,000)

- Procurement of approximately 900,000 ITNs for 2017 mass campaign. ($3,213,000)

- Support the distribution of ITNs, including transportation and other logistics, to districts and health facilities. ($500,000)

- Provide technical assistance for the continuous distribution channels for sustaining high ITN coverage in selected provinces/districts to ensure channels can be scaled up following 2017-2018 mass distribution campaign. ($150,000)

- Monitor the durability and physical integrity of ITNs following the 2017 mass campaign. (see M&E section)

- Provide CDC technical assistance for routine monitoring of net durability. (see M&E section)

- Support BCC activities to increase consistent utilization of ITNs. (see BCC section)

2. Indoor residual spraying

NMCP/PMI objectives

The NMCP/PMI collaboration aims to provide access to evidence-based vector control to 100% of households and persons at risk in targeted areas by 2016. IRS is recognized as the only intervention available to manage insecticide resistance through rotation among different classes of WHOPES-approved insecticides, making entomological monitoring an indispensable component of an evidence-based resistance management program.

The updated Zambian National Malaria Strategic Plan for 2011–2016 has the goal of achieving universal coverage with ITNs. According to the WHO, IRS is the preferred vector control intervention as part of an insecticide resistance management strategy in areas where there is documented resistance to pyrethroids. Otherwise, IRS will be a key addition to ITNs in specifically targeted densely populated areas. The primary integrated vector management objectives of the NMSP are to cover at least 85 percent of all targeted structures by the end of 2016 with malaria case surveillance-driven IRS, and to have at least 80 percent of people living in malaria risk areas using appropriate malaria prevention and control interventions by 2016.

The NMCP is using other partners for small-scale larviciding projects in Lusaka and has not requested PMI for support.

Progress since PMI was launched

Zambia is implementing IRS for malaria control as part of an integrated vector management strategy. The modern history of IRS in Zambia began when the Government of the Republic of Zambia (GRZ) started spraying again in 2003 following the success of IRS by the private sector, specifically, at the Konkola Copper Mines in the Copperbelt Province and later at Zambia Sugar Company in the town of Mazabuka in Southern Province. IRS is one of the key malaria control strategies of the NMCP.

The Government of Zambia has in recent years been increasing resource allocation to malaria control in general and IRS in particular. In 2013 the MOH procured $10 million worth of organophosphate for IRS in non-PMI supported areas. Additional resources and technical support have been mobilized through a number of external partners, including PMI, DFID, the Roll Back Malaria partnership, the Global Fund for HIV/AIDS, Tuberculosis and Malaria (Global Fund), the World Bank's Malaria Booster Project, and WHO.

In 2010, Zambia reported insecticide resistance to three of the four insecticide classes recommended by the WHO for vector control. High levels of resistance were reported to DDT, carbamates, and pyrethroids, which were the main insecticides in use at that time for controlling malaria. Initial geographic coverage of resistance data was limited to nine districts in three provinces surrounding the capital of Lusaka. Therefore, the potential for vector control failure was high. PMI supported the NMCP to establish an insecticide resistance management technical working group and enhanced efforts to monitor both insecticide resistance and the resistance mechanisms present in the country. This information was compiled to develop an insecticide resistance management (IRM) plan in accordance with the WHO Global Plan for Insecticide Resistance Management of malaria vectors.

Table G: PMI-supported IRS activities 2006 - 2015

Calendar Year	Number of Districts Sprayed	Insecticide Used	Number of Structures Sprayed	Coverage Rate	Population Protected
2006	15	DDT and pyrethroids	592,346	85%	—
2007	15	DDT and pyrethroids	657,695	93%	—
2008	36	DDT and pyrethroids	1,100,000	90%	—
2009	36	DDT and pyrethroids	1,300,000	90%	—
2010	54	DDT and pyrethroids	1,300,000	89%	5,500,000
2011	35	Carbamates and pyrethroids	1,200,000	83%	6,200,000
2012	20	Carbamates and organophosphates	460,303	86%	1,710,833
2013	20	Organophosphates	432,398	81%	1,842,821
2014	40***	Organophosphates	409,544	93%	2,000,824
2015*	40***	Organophosphates	482,077 (target)	TBD	2,141,077 (target)
2016**	36	TBD	400,000	TBD	TBD
2017**	36	TBD	400,000	TBD	TBD

*Represents targets based on the draft 2015 IRS work plan.
** Represents projected targets based on national strategic plan and/or discussions with the NMCP.
*** Includes DFID-funded districts

Progress during the last 12-18 months

In FY 2015, PMI supported the NMCP IRS operations in 25 PMI focus districts (9 in Eastern Province; 7 in Muchinga Province and 9 in Northern Province). An additional 15 districts in Luapula and Central Provinces were sprayed using DFID funding (11 in Luapula Province and four in Central Province). Among the 40 districts that PMI sprayed (Figure 5), the IRS implementation start dates were staggered weekly due to the number of districts to be supervised. Districts with the largest number of structures were sprayed first. Approximately 409,544 structures were sprayed, out of the targeted 438,252 (93% coverage) protecting more than 2 million people. The 2014 spray round lasted 65 days. DFID support for IRS in the 15 districts will end at the end of calendar year 2015.

Figure 5: PMI and DFID Supported Districts - Old boundary districts

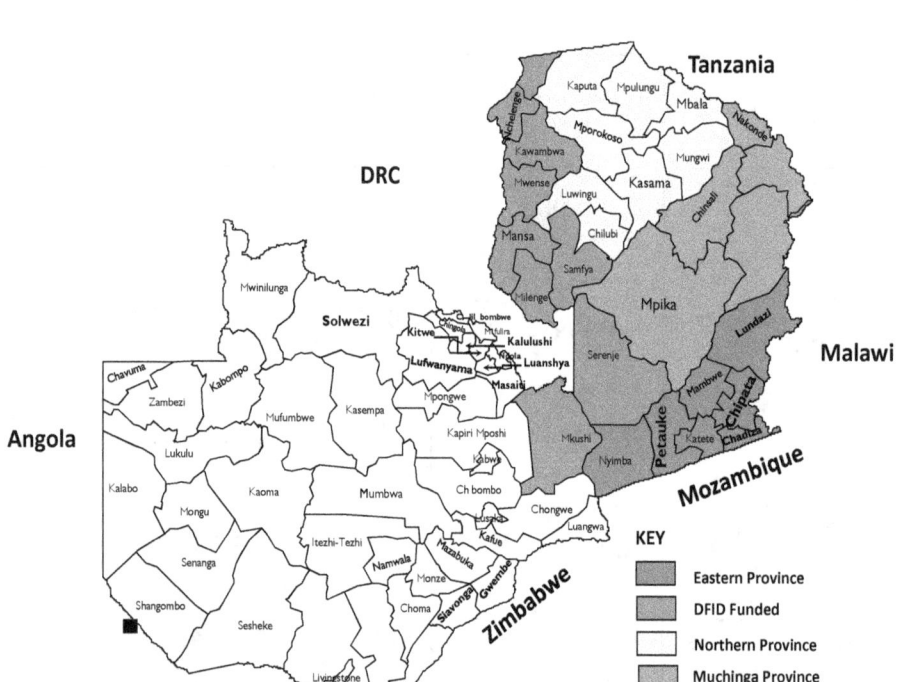

The IRS program was conducted in compliance with United States Government's USAID Regulation 216, Zambia Environmental Management Act cap 204, No 12 of 2011, and USAID Initial and Supplemental Environmental Assessments and Pesticide Evaluation Report and Safer Use Action Plan and its amendments. During October–December 2014, pre- and mid-spray environmental compliance inspections were conducted in the 40 target districts, as was random inspection of houses sprayed to check for quality of messages to homeowners after the spray. End-of-day clean-ups and triple rinsing practice to check for liquid waste management checks were also carried out. Post-spray inventories in all 40 districts were conducted during February–March 2015; all districts carried out clean-ups at time of inspection. An insecticide inventory verified good stock control in all sites.

The MOH committed significant funding towards IRS in 2014. With funding from the Government of Zambia, the NMCP conducted IRS in 43 non-PMI supported districts using organophosphates. The NMCP has sufficient left over insecticides from the 2014 spraying season for use in the 43 districts during the 2015 spray season. PMI provides technical support to the NMCP for environmental compliance including waste disposal, entomology and planning for IRS activities in the non PMI supported provinces.

The criteria for selection of areas to be sprayed at district level were previously not clear. The policy change for IRS, which was implemented in 2011, entailed developing criteria for targeting areas at sub district level to be sprayed. In 2014 PMI piloted targeted IRS in 15 districts in Luapula (11) and Central (4) Provinces using satellite-based enumeration of eligible structures overlaid with HMIS data. In 2015, targeted IRS will again be conducted in the same 15 districts.

During the 2014 season, long-lasting organophosphates were used across the whole country. Bioassays were conducted to assess the quality of spraying in the target districts. All bioassays conducted within 48 hours of spraying in November 2014, recorded 100% mortalities of susceptible Kisumu strain *An. gambiae* s.s. Three months post-IRS, average percentage mortalities of 100% were still being recorded. By the seventh month post IRS, mortality ranged between 38% to 94% on mud walls and 50% to 100% on cement walls.

Insecticide resistance to available IRS chemicals continues to pose a threat to the IRS program. PMI supported the NMCP to develop a National Insecticide Resistance Management Plan (2014-2017) that calls for periodic, but evidence-based, scheduled rotation of insecticides used in the IRS program. The plan recommends that: 1) Pyrethroids should no longer be used for IRS, until local insecticide resistance monitoring demonstrates that the high levels of pyrethroid resistance have declined in the vector population; 2) Although organophosphates are still effective for IRS in Zambia, the NMCP should consider rotating to DDT in 2015 or 2016 as a means of managing resistance to organophosphates; 3) The NMCP needs to continue to monitor resistance at each sentinel site twice a year, before and after spraying; 4) Going forward, aim to rotate insecticide in all areas informed by monitoring data and should include a combination of OP, DDT, and carbamates. In addition, with PMI assistance, the MOH/NMCC developed a more complete map of insecticide resistance in the country. Previous insecticide resistance surveys have reported resistance in the two major malaria vector species, *An. gambiae* and *An. funestus*. A recent survey conducted in 2013-2014 reported *An. gambiae* resistance to pyrethroids throughout Zambia. Resistance to bendiocarb (a carbamate) was found, particularly in areas of Luapula and Northern provinces. DDT resistance was also widespread. *An. funestus* was reported to be largely susceptible to DDT but resistant to pyrethroids throughout the country. *An. funestus* populations in the Eastern Province were shown to be resistant to bendiocarb. However, all vector species were found to be susceptible to organophosphates. Identity of the insecticide to be used after organophosphates will depend upon resistance surveillance data particularly that obtained with the intensity bioassay. The current insecticide resistance status is provided in Figure 6.

Figure 6. Insecticide resistance status

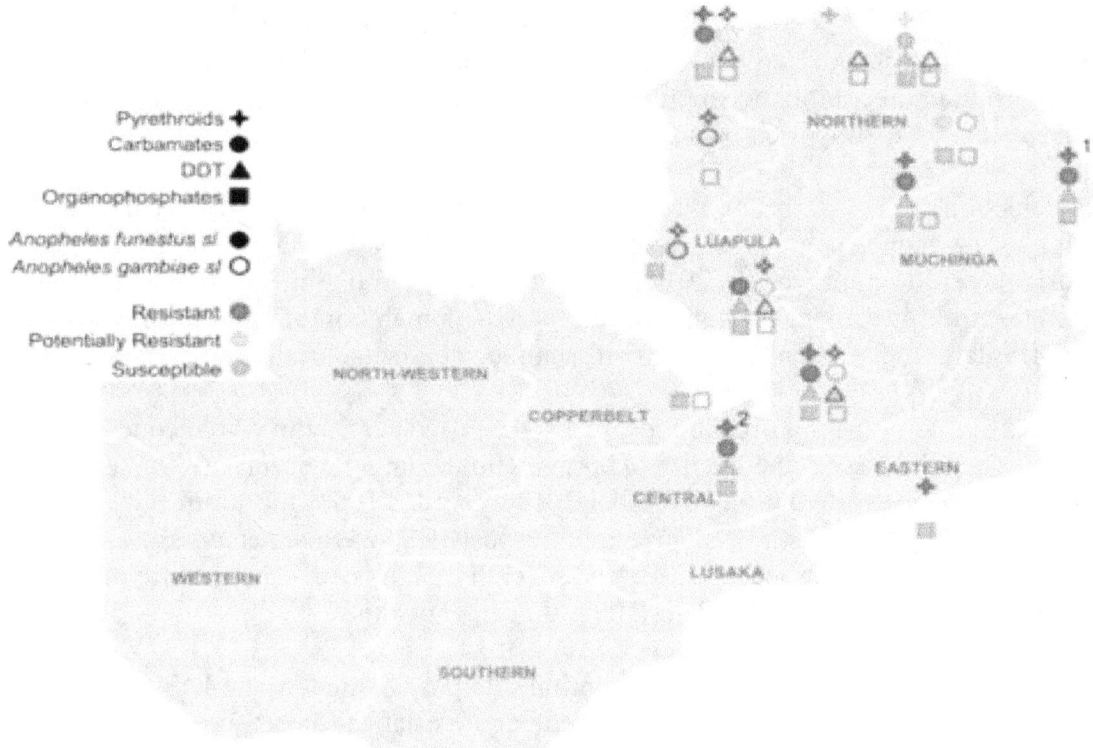

A lab facility has been identified on the NMCC campus that can be developed at little cost into an associated PCR, LAMP, and intensity bioassay facility. This will allow determination of vector species and details of resistance intensity and mechanism(s), and through application of the intensity resistance assay to detect instances of control failure to be accomplished in Zambia within the NMCP/PMI collaboration. An OR project assessing the intensity bioassay has been funded for implementation in Zambia.

A new pre-fabricated insectary, procured with PMI funds, is now operational at the NMCC campus. This facility will strengthen both IRS and ITN assessment capability.

Zambia has been included in the recently awarded Next Generation Indoor Residual Spraying (NGenIRS) Project (2016-2019) as a year one country. NGenIRS is a UNITAID-funded partnership between the Innovative Vector Control Consortium (IVCC), PMI, Global Fund, PATH/MACEPA, and NMCPs, with the overall aim of accelerating and expanding access to and adoption of the new, third generation of indoor residual spraying (3GIRS) formulations that overcome insecticide resistance and increase the effective lifetime of IRS products. The goal of the NGenIRS project is sustainable and rational deployment of effective malaria vector control tools in insecticide resistance management programs to save lives and improve health. As a consequence of the NgenIRS project, PMI will be able to procure organophosphates at reduced cost resulting in savings that will benefit continued IRS support to Luapula in 2017.

Plans and justification

For the 2017 spray season, PMI will cover the cost of IRS in up to 36 districts in three provinces: Eastern, Muchinga, and Northern. Approximately 400,000 structures will be targeted, protecting approximately 2 million people. The actual number of household/structures sprayed will depend on the cost of insecticides selected, and the cost of implementation. The incidence of the disease at sub district level will inform selection of areas for IRS.

Planned activities also include expanded insecticide resistance monitoring and management, entomological monitoring, and support of environmental assessments. Specific activities include: pre-season environmental compliance inspection; collection of empty plastics bottles generated from the previous spray campaign; support to rehabilitation of IRS facilities such as soak pits, shower rooms and change rooms; support for MOH/NMCC and MCDMCH to conduct training of trainers for spray operators; preparing a "Letter Report" for environmental compliance; launching spray operations in up to 36 districts; carrying out periodic testing of vector population for phenotypic resistance; carrying out pre-spray vector population density determination in PMI supported sentinel sites; supporting NMCP teams to carry out monitoring and supervision during IRS implementation; procurement of insecticide, spray pumps, PPE, and other IRS commodities.

The six PMI supported sentinel sites will be retained for 2017 entomological surveillance activities (Table H). However, this level of surveillance alone is insufficient for resistance management decision-making. The most efficient expansion of surveillance is to use the current sites to anchor transects of 50 to 100 km that allow for assessments to be conducted on how representative the sentinel sites are and provide information on resistance hot-spots. Additionally, other entomologic metrics that influence resistance management decisions will be captured for these transects. PMI will review surveillance activities with the NMCP and stakeholders during the IRM TWG meeting in September 2015. Molecular species identification with appropriate timeliness will be provided by CDC Entomology Branch until the NMCC lab refurbishment and training of NMCC personnel are complete, a rebooting required by the loss of key entomology personnel. Existing assistance of Macha Malaria Research Institute in species determinations will also continue when it is possible for the work to be done in a timely way. PMI will take every opportunity to include other entomological monitoring activities being undertaken in Zambia, for example those conducted as a part of the PMI intensity assay OR project or data collected by other entities working in Zambia.

Table H. PMI Supported Entomological Surveillance Sentinel Sites

District	Province
Katete	Eastern
Serenje	Central
Kasama	Northern
Isoka	Muchinga
Mwense and Milenge	Luapula

PMI supports the MOH policy to rotate the insecticide used for IRS, based on evidence of vector resistance to insecticides. The recommendation from the Insecticide Resistance Management

Technical Advisory Committee is to consider rotating to DDT in 2016 in selected districts. PMI will explore the feasibility of using DDT in the Eastern province in the 2017 spray round. In most of southern Africa, *An. funestus* has been traditionally highly susceptible to DDT. However, there have been recent reports from South African researchers of DDT resistance in *An. funestus* collections from eastern Zambia which will be an issue to consider.

Proposed activities with FY 2016 funding: ($8,323,500)

- Procure insecticides (i.e., organophosphates and/or a non-pyrethroid insecticide based on the most recent insecticide resistance data) and other IRS supplies/equipment for spraying up to 400,000 structures in 36 districts, inclusive of districts previously supported by DFID. Support environmental monitoring and environmental assessment, to include use of DDT, organophosphates, or carbamates. ($6,170,500)

- Train spray operators, supervisors, and store keepers; monitoring and evaluation; BCC for IRS; pesticide storage; waste disposal; and pay for spray operations in 36 PMI-funded districts. ($1,674,000)

- Support entomological monitoring, including providing support to NMCP to build entomological capacity and continue insecticide resistance management. ($450,000)

- Provide CDC technical assistance for entomological monitoring and insecticide resistance management. ($29,000)

3. Malaria in pregnancy

NMCP/PMI objectives

In 2014, the NMCP aligned the national policy on IPTp with the recently updated WHO policy on IPTp. The national policy now calls for pregnant women to receive IPTp at every ANC visit, at least one month apart up to the time of delivery with the first dose starting after 16 weeks of gestation. Iron and 5mg folate are also provided to pregnant women through ante-natal care. The MCDH and MOH are yet to agree on a common position regarding folic acid supplementation. MCDMCH has already included low dose folic acid in the draft revised Focused Antenatal Care Guidelines. However, MOH still maintains that folic acid should be given at current (5mg) dose. PMI/Zambia continues to advocate for low dose folic acid with the MOH. Technical working groups meet regularly to move forward the malaria in pregnancy agenda in Zambia. These groups include representatives from the MOH, MCDMCH, and various malaria and reproductive health partners including PMI.

In partnership with the NMCP, PMI supports three main strategies to address malaria in pregnancy: IPTp, ITNs, and case management. ITNs are procured and distributed directly to pregnant women through ANC clinics and also are accessible to them through additional distribution channels (mass campaigns, and continuous school-based and community-based channels, as discussed in the ITN section, above). PMI also supports appropriate case management of malaria in pregnancy through trainings of healthcare workers on malaria diagnosis and treatment guidelines (see the Case Management section below for details).

Progress since PMI was launched

IPTp is a MOH, MCDMCH and RBM intervention for preventing malaria in pregnancy. Since 2004, Zambia, has promoted the WHO Focused Antenatal Care (FANC); IPTp is an important part of this approach to reduce maternal and newborn mortality and morbidity including from stillbirths and premature delivery. Over the past nine years, PMI has invested approximately $3 million in FANC/MIP in Zambia, where the 2014 annual number of births was 608 per 1000. Funding from PMI has been critical to the development of the national FANC curriculum; development of district-level trainers throughout the country; the national rollout of in-service trainings in FANC; updating the pre-service curriculum in nursing schools in Zambia; strengthening supervision and quality improvement of ANC services; and creating demand for quality ANC services and advocating for safe motherhood issues. PMI funds were complemented with MCH co-funding in line with the program's budget.

Progress during the last 12-18 months

Focused antenatal care is a comprehensive prenatal care package provided to pregnant women at ANC clinics that includes care related to malaria such as providing SP, providing an ITN at the first ANC visit, and educating pregnant women on the importance of seeking care immediately for fever. FANC training and supervision is provided to healthcare workers via clinical care teams (CCTs) present in all districts and provinces nationwide. These teams consist of staff who are already part of the health system, namely a clinical care supervisor and a CHW coordinator. Provincial-level CCTs supervise and train CCTs and health workers at district-level facilities. District-level CCTs train and supervise health workers at the local facility level. PMI supports the malaria in pregnancy component of training for the CCTs. As of the end of FY 2014, 504 health workers in 27 targeted old boundary districts across all provinces received training on FANC.

Because the availability of SP is critical for IPTp, PMI has continued to invest in EMLIP to improve distribution of malaria commodities (see Treatment and Pharmaceutical Management section) and to prevent stockouts of malaria commodities in facilities. Availability of SP in ANC clinics has improved due to these investments.

SP resistance continues to be monitored as a threat to the efficacy of IPTp. A PMI-funded study[5] analyzed the efficacy of SP for IPTp in Mansa, Zambia in 2013. This study found a 26% parasitological failure rate for IPTp-SP relative to the moderate 61% prevalence of the quintuple mutant among pregnant women with asymptomatic malaria parasitemia. The threat of SP resistance looms, and continuous resistance monitoring is needed especially in light of the emergence of the sextuple mutation, but IPTp-SP seems to retain some degree of efficacy in Mansa. Although the study cannot be generalized for Zambian women nationwide, this provides evidence that IPTp is still effective in the study population of Zambian women.

---

[5] Tan et al. Malaria Journal 2014, 13:227 http://www.malariajournal.com/content/13/1/227

National BCC efforts for MIP are now part of a larger integrated campaign on maternal health and nutrition that disseminates messages through national radio and television spots encouraging early prenatal care, use of nets during pregnancy, and the importance of IPTp. Community BCC efforts focus on educating and training SMAGs, where they are present; MIP; and other aspects of ANC. Other community BCC activities related to MIP were also supported by PMI in FY 2014 (see BCC section). Since 2011, PMI has been supporting the implementation of integrated community-based communications initiative called "Champion Communities" that focuses on promotion of malaria prevention, diagnosis, and appropriate treatment. The objectives of the initiative include having all pregnant women in the community attend ANC early and receive the recommended doses of IPTp. The initiative is being implemented in 8 districts and 131 communities across 4 higher malaria burden provinces. A recent monitoring and evaluation report of the "Champion communities" approach showed an increase in ANC attendance, from 52% at the baseline in 2013 to 96% in 2014. The first dose of IPTp uptake was close to 100% in 2014 in the targeted communities.

Commodity gap analysis

Table I. SP Gap Analysis for Malaria in Pregnancy

Calendar Year	2015	2016	2017
Total Population	15,031,200	15,452,074	15,884,732
SP Needs			
Total number of pregnant women attending ANC	758,174	779,403	801,227
Total SP Need (in treatments)	**1,971,253**	**2,026,448**	**2,083,190**
Partner Contributions			
SP carried over from previous year	1,838,618	3,010,032	983,584
SP from MOH	3,142,667	0	1,100,000
SP from Global Fund	0	0	0
SP from Other Donors	0	0	0
SP planned with PMI funding	0	0	0
Total SP Available	4,981,285	3,010,032	2,083,584
Total SP Surplus (Gap)	3,010,032	983,584	394

Notes: Population growth is estimated at 2.8% and based on 2010 population census data. Approximately 5.2% of national population is pregnant mothers. Total antenatal attendance estimated at 97% in 2014. 95.0% of pregnant mothers attending antenatal clinics will receive first IPTp dose, 80% will receive second IPTp dose and 65% will receive the third IPTp dose. 20% of the total antenatal attendances visit the health facilities at the right time (fourth month of pregnancy) and are likely to receive the fourth IPTp dose in 2014. This assumption was applied for 2015 to 2017.

Plans and justification

The strategy to increase IPTp coverage in Zambia includes targeting rural areas. PMI will continue to support supervision and training of health center clinical staff in FANC in the updated policies through CCTs. The newly-trained district level CCTs will focus their initial training and supervisory visits on rural facilities. Because cultural and knowledge barriers resulting in decreased uptake of IPTp will require continued BCC regarding IPTp, PMI will continue to make investments in BCC to prevent MIP (see BCC section).

To improve patient knowledge and demand for prevention and treatment of malaria in pregnancy, PMI will continue to support national- and community-level BCC activities, with an emphasis on local BCC activities such as SMAGs in rural areas.

Proposed activities with FY 2016 funding: ($300,000)

- Training provincial and district level health workers on then updated NMCP IPTp guidelines in four high malaria burden provinces (Luapula, Muchinga, Northern, and Eastern). These four provinces constitute 36 high burden malaria districts. ($300,000)

- National and community BCC efforts for MIP will include messages through national and local radio, national television spots, and SMAGs encouraging timely ANC attendance, encouraging ANC visits during pregnancy, use of nets during pregnancy, and updated IPTp recommendations. (see BCC section)

4. Case management

a. Diagnosis and Treatment

NMCP/PMI objectives

The *Guidelines for the Diagnosis and Treatment of Malaria in Zambia (Fourth Edition 2014)* are aligned with the revised 2010 WHO recommendations on universal diagnostic testing for malaria. The NMSP Strategic Plan 2011–2016 diagnostic objective is to ensure all suspected malaria cases receive parasitological confirmation by 2016. Parasitological confirmation is done by examining either a blood smear/slide by microscopy or malaria RDT. Antimalarial treatment based on a clinical diagnosis should only be considered when a parasitological diagnosis is not immediately available.

Microscopy should be used where there is a well-functioning laboratory with staff well-trained in malaria diagnostics. RDTs are to be used in health facilities where there is no microscopy or no well-trained laboratory staff, when a laboratory is closed or too busy to handle the work load and at the community level by CHWs trained in iCCM.

Regarding malaria case management, all suspected malaria cases shall be subjected to parasite-based diagnosis and treatment initiated in accordance with the test result. The first-line drug for treatment of uncomplicated malaria in Zambia is artemether-lumefantrine (AL). A recent addition to the treatment guidelines is dihydroartemisin-piperaquine (DHA-PQ) as an alternative first-line choice for uncomplicated malaria. For uncomplicated malaria in pregnancy, the first-line treatments are quinine in the first trimester and AL in the second and third trimesters.

The treatment of severe malaria was updated in 2014. Injectable artesunate is the drug of choice in adults and children; if injectable (intravenous-IV or intramuscular-IM) artesunate is unavailable, artemether (IM) or quinine (IV or IM) are suggested alternatives. The national malaria treatment and diagnostic guidelines recommend that patients with severe malaria receive pre-referral treatment with IM or rectal artesunate; if that is not available, then IM quinine is recommended. The guidelines state that the treatment of severe malaria in pregnancy is with quinine in the first trimester and injectable artesunate in the second and third trimesters.

Progress since PMI was launched

The NMCP, PMI, and partners have invested in three key areas related to malaria diagnostics: 1) procurement and distribution of diagnostic commodities; 2) training of clinical and laboratory personnel in the use of malaria diagnostic tools; and 3) training of national, provincial, and district level staff in providing outreach training and supportive supervision (OTSS) for quality assurance of malaria diagnostics.

This investment is having an impact. The percentage of children with fever that reported having a heel or finger stick increased from 17% (MIS 2010) to 32% (MIS 2012). The HMIS confirms progress in diagnostics (Figure 7). Sixty-six percent of reported malaria cases were confirmed in 2014, compared with 31% in 2010, and 78% were confirmed nationally in the first quarter of 2015 (HMIS).

Figure 7. Diagnostic Confirmation Trend Total Malaria Cases in Zambia, 2010 - 2015 (Q1)

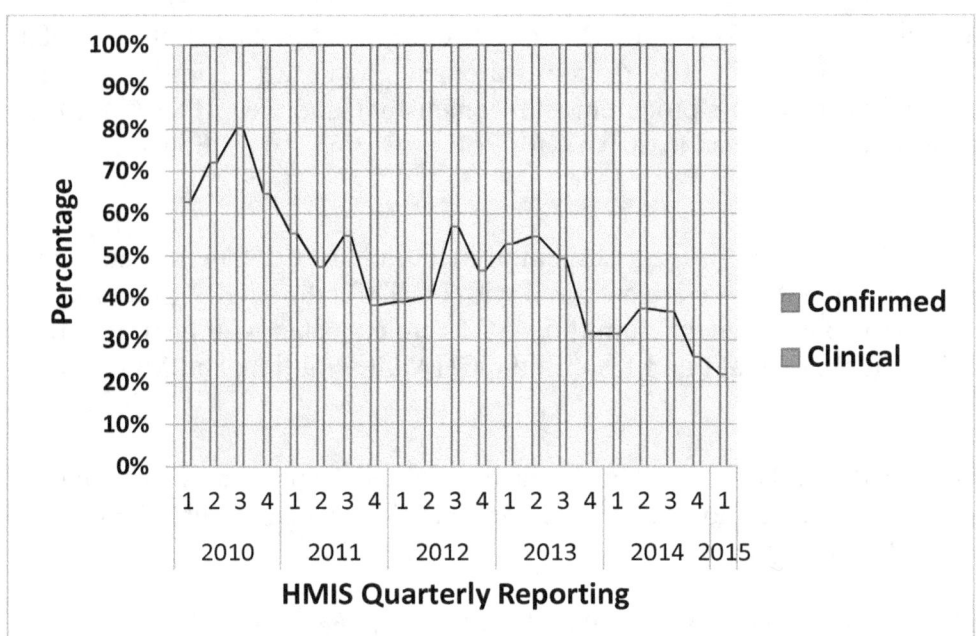

The RDT supply has improved. The PMI EUV survey for the first quarter of FY 2015 reported RDT stockouts in only one facility out of the 40 visited.

To strengthen malaria diagnostic capacity at all levels, PMI has invested in training laboratory technicians, clinicians, and CHWs in malaria diagnosis— supporting health workers in approximately 18 facilities in each of the 10 provinces in the country and training over 1,400 CHWs in iCCM and over 2,300 clinicians. According to the national *Health Sector Human Resources Strategic Plan (2011-2016)*, Zambia has 1,535 clinical officers, 911 medical doctors, 2,671 midwives and 7,669 nurses. Training for clinicians includes training in national malaria diagnosis and treatment guidelines, training in IPTp, and case management in pregnancy, as well as refresher trainings. There are more than 23,000 community volunteers in Zambia. Information on how many of these are CHWs is not readily available. All cadres listed above are targeted for training. PMI supported the development and distribution of a laboratory training manual with standard operating procedures, the WHO accreditation of three laboratory technicians at the national level to build microscopy expertise and training capacity, and diagnostics refresher training for 18 district laboratory supervisors.

To ensure quality of malaria diagnostics and adherence to test results, PMI supports the OTSS program. In OTSS, provincial and district-level supervisors visit health facilities using standardized checklists to observe microscopy and RDTs, recheck malaria smears, and collect information on provider adherence to laboratory results. These supervisors also provide on-site training and corrective action as needed.

Progress during the last 12-18 months

In 2014 there were no national level stockouts of RDTs or ACTs reported in the country. A total of 17.4 million RDTs arrived in Zambia in 2014 from procurements by GRZ (5.5 million), PMI (4 million), DFID (7.4 million using PMI's procurement mechanisms), and the CHAZ (243,000). In 2015, over 19 million RDTs are expected to arrive with PMI providing 1.6 million and DFID procuring 5 million.

PMI procured 3.4 million ACTs in 2014 for the treatment of malaria in health facilities and in the community. In addition, 3.5 million ACTs were procured with DFID funding; GRZ procured over 11 million ACTs. In 2015 approximately 20 million ACTs are expected with PMI providing over 4 million, DFID 1.59 million, Global Fund 1.6 million, CHAZ 2.9 million, and MOH over 8.9 million.

Through March 2015, 466 health workers in 110 health facilities in all 10 provinces participated in OTSS. PMI is also supporting the development of a comprehensive and sustainable national malaria diagnostics QA/QC framework.

In 2014, the NMCP and partners made revisions to the *Guidelines for the Diagnosis and Treatment of Malaria in Zambia* that included: injectable artesunate for severe malaria, DHA-PQ as an alternate first-line treatment of uncomplicated malaria, and rectal artesunate for pre-referral treatment of severe malaria, although this is yet to be rolled out. PMI partnered with CHAI for the phased roll-out of injectable artesunate for severe malaria. CHAI supported the trainings at 1 tertiary facility and 19 secondary facilities while PMI provided the artesunate commodity and technical assistance. Going forward, the Ministry of Health has committed to procuring injectable artesunate.

AL remains efficacious in Zambia, as observed in a Drug Efficacy Study (DES) conducted by the NMCP in 2012.[6] The NMCP aims to conduct DESs regularly to ensure the efficacy of first-line malaria drugs. The PMI-supported DES that was planned for the first quarter of FY 2015 has been delayed until fourth quarter FY 2015. This DES will include AL, ASAQ, and DHA-PQ. PMI does not plan to support a DES with FY 2016 funds.

PMI supports training and supervision of healthcare workers. In FY 2014, 324 health workers in all provinces received training in malaria case management with ACTs including the training of 503 CHWs in iCCM. The NMCP conducts supervision through a cascade approach. The MOH through the NMCC provides training to the provincial level, including provincial hospitals. MCDMCH provides training at the district level and below. Supervision was supported via training of CCTs on supervisory skills specific to malaria case management. CCTs provided supervision for case management of malaria, with provincial level teams supervising district staffs, who in turn supervise staff at local health facilities. The OTSS program supported by PMI also works to improve adherence to test results and increase compliance with diagnostic and treatment algorithms for management of fever.

---

[6] Busiku Hamainza, Moonga Hawela, Pascalina Chanda, Victor Chalwe, Fred Masaninga and Mulakwa Kamuliwo (2013). *Therapeutic efficacy testing for artemether- lumefantrine – Chipata and Katete sites.* Lusaka: National Malaria Control Center.

Commodity gap analysis

Table J: RDT Gap Analysis

Calendar Year	2015	2016	2017
RDT Needs			
Target population at risk for malaria	15,031,200	15,452,074	15,884,732
Total number projected fever cases	19,211,065	19,748,975	20,301,947
Percent of fever cases confirmed with microscopy	20	10	10
Percent of fever cases confirmed with RDT	80	90	90
Total RDT Needs	**19,211,065**	**17,774,078**	**18,271,752**
Partner Contributions			
RDTs carried over from previous year	3,551,343	5,590,583	0
RDTs from MOH	12,416,740	10,000,000	10,000,000
RDTs from Global Fund	3,211,065	494,975	6,068,284
RDTs from Other Donors	4,000,000	0	0
RDTs planned with PMI funding	1,622,500	1,000,000	2,500,000
Total RDTs Available	**24,801,648**	**17,085,558**	**18,568,284**
Total RDT Surplus (Gap)	**5,590,583**	**(688,520)**	**296,532**

Notes: OPD attendance was 21,668,763 in 2012. Applying a 15% increment; it was assumed that OPD attendance will increase to 28,656,939 in 2014 and 32,955,480 in 2015. The same assumption was applied to 2016 and 2017.Based on data from the EUV for the period October 2012 to December 2014, it is assumed that 58% of OPD attendance will present with fever as a clinical symptom. RDT need for 2015 is inclusive of 3 months buffer of 3,842,213 RDTs.

Table K: ACT Gap Analysis

Calendar Year	2015	2016	2017
ACT Needs			
Target population at risk for malaria	15,031,200	15,452,074	15,884,732
Total projected number of malaria cases	5,000,000	4,500,000	4,000,000
Total ACT Needs	**16,154,053**	**11,808,972**	**10,746,165**
Partner Contributions			
ACTs carried over from previous year	488,800	3,250,139	3,250,139
ACTs from MOH	8,984,250	6,000,000	3,000,000
ACTs from Global Fund	3,133,242	2,808,972	1,120,000
ACTs from Other Donors	2,591,900	0	0
ACTs planned with PMI funding	4,206,000	3,000,000	3,300,000
Total ACTs Available	19,404,192	15,059,111	10,670,139
Total ACT Surplus (Gap)	3,250,139	3,250,139	(76,026)

Notes: Needs for ACTs are calculated based on "consumption" as reported by the 17 EMLIP districts and extrapolated to the rest of the country, and includes the need for a buffer stock to prevent stockouts. The total ACT need in 2015 is inclusive of 3 months buffer of 3,230,811 treatment courses. A 10% decline of inpatient cases per year is anticipated.

Plans and justification

The NMCP has prioritized technical support for case management for PMI support. HMIS data has shown progressive improvement in malaria diagnosis confirmation. Confirmed malaria cases accounted for 78% of total malaria cases in the second quarter of 2015 up from 68% during the same period in 2014 and 47% in 2013. Furthermore, the MIS 2012 indicated that among children under five with fever that received an anti-malarial drug, 85% reported receiving the recommended antimalarial (AL) up from 18% in 2006.

According to the 2012 MIS, the private sector accounted for 13.8% of children who received anti-malarials for treatment of malaria while Government health facilities accounted for 73.9%. The private health care sector in Zambia is small, accounting for 14% of all health facilities and are found mostly in Lusaka and Copperbelt province were malaria incidence is low.

Thus, the priority going forward for PMI will be to improve diagnostics and supportive supervision and expand access to treatment through iCCM. With FY 2016 funding, PMI will work to increase prompt and effective treatment for uncomplicated malaria at the health facility level and support efforts to expand malaria treatment at the community level utilizing CHWs.

To provide health care workers, laboratory technicians, and CHWs with the tools to diagnose malaria, PMI will continue to support the procurement of malaria diagnostic commodities. PMI will procure RDTs for use in health facilities and by CHWs. Also, reagents for microscopy will be provided for use by trained laboratory technicians at targeted facilities.

PMI will continue to support OTSS at targeted facilities as well as refresher training. Health facilities performance for malaria diagnosis and treatment will be monitored through OTSS. Health facilities whose performance shows significant improvement will be transitioned to receiving fewer OTSS visits. Additional facilities will then be selected to receive OTSS. Selection of additional health facilities for OTSS going forward will be based on diagnostic performance. High volume and low performance facilities will be targeted. PMI will also strengthen the quality of parasitological diagnosis in the public health sector in four provinces through supportive supervision of healthcare providers at primary health facilities and community levels.

Proposed activities with FY 2016 funding: ($5,930,000)

- Procure 2,500,000 RDTs to be used at health facilities and by CHWs to contribute towards filling the RDT need in 2017. ($960,000)

- Strengthen malaria diagnostic capacity and quality assurance centrally and in areas outside the four higher malaria burden provinces through the training of malaria microscopists and support for OTSS. ($400,000)

- Improve the quality of parasitological diagnosis in the public sector in four targeted provinces through training and supportive supervision of healthcare providers at PHC and community levels. PMI will work at the provincial, district, and community level to improve the appropriate use of diagnostics including interpreting test results and managing patients based on results. This activity will begin during FY 2015 and expand to additional health facilities and the community with FY 2016 funding. ($400,000)

- Procure microscopes, reagents and supplies to equip health centers for their malaria microscopy needs (417 health facilities have laboratories with microscopy). ($70,000)

- Procure approximately 3,300,000 treatment courses of AL for uncomplicated malaria and Semi-annual quantifications will monitor the supply and demand. ($3,300,000)

- Support the supervision of healthcare providers in the treatment of uncomplicated malaria and the training of CHWs in iCCM in four targeted provinces. Also, support the training of health workers at health facilities with inpatient services on the use of injectable artesunate for severe malaria. ($700,000)

- Fund BCC messages and activities to increase utilization and acceptance of diagnostics and to promote use of and adherence to recommended quality-assured ACTs. (see full description under the BCC section, below)

b. Pharmaceutical Management

NMCP/PMI objectives

The National Supply Chain Strategy for Essential Medicines (2015-2020) aims to provide equitable access to affordable, quality essential medicines and medical supplies to support the Zambian public health system. Key strategies of the MOH's strategic plan to achieve this objective include the following:

- Establish a coordinated and efficient supply chain in the [health] sector led by one lead entity/point of reference.
- Reduce shortages of medical commodities and supplies within the supply chain by increasing the fill rate from the current 50% to 80%.
- Improve access to medical commodities and supplies though decentralizing distribution.
- Enhance accuracy in quantification and forecasting of medical commodities and supplies within the sector through provision of accurate data.
- Mobilize resources to support supply chain interventions in the sector
- Ensure sustained and improved quality for all medical commodities and supplies within the public health sector.
- Attain dynamic supply chain alignment and agility within the public health sector.
- Improve decision making processes through timely provision of information across the supply chain, by implementing appropriate supply chain information systems and technologies.
- Ensure private sector participation in the public health sector through various initiatives including Public Private Partnerships (PPPs).

During the strategic planning process, key supply chain objectives were grouped and defined into the following pillars that provide the framework around which the strategic objectives were formulated:

- Quantification
- Procurement
- Logistics
- Information Systems
- Quality assurance and rational use
- Commodity security, financing and resource mobilization
- Performance management
- Human resources for health in supply chain
- Public Private Partnerships

In late 2012, the MOH announced the mandate of the Medical Stores Limited (MSL) would be significantly increased. In the past, MSL was responsible for central-level storage of commodities and distribution of those commodities to the district. Districts were then responsible for further distribution to health centers. The new policy expands MSL's mandate to include distribution to the health center. In order to expand its capacity for last mile distribution, MSL has created three regional hubs and staging posts throughout the country. MSL's revised mandate also includes taking on roles that were previously the responsibility of the MOH's Procurement and Supply Unit. These roles include procurement, procurement planning, and quantification of essential medicines and medical supplies. The transfer of these activities were originally planned to be completed in 2014. However, the transfer of these activities has been put on hold as MSL builds its capacity as well as develops a comprehensive strategic plan for its expanded mandate.

Progress since PMI was launched

PMI has invested in three key areas related to commodity security: logistics systems strengthening, procurement and distribution of malaria commodities; conducting of EUV surveys to ensure adherence to both diagnostic and treatment guidelines; and training of facility staff, district and central level supervisors in EMLIP.[7]

PMI has supported the Government of Zambia in developing the National Supply Chain Strategy for Essential Medicines including malaria commodities (2015–2020). The strategy is aimed at ensuring to equitable access to affordable, quality essential medicines and medical supplies to support the Zambian public health system. The investment has contributed to ensuring commodity security for all malaria commodities. This has been achieved through conducting transparent and coordinated forecasting and quantification

In recent years, the Government of Zambia has been increasing resource allocation to procurement of malaria commodities. In 2013, the MOH allocated $24 million towards procured of malaria commodities. The funding increased to $27 million and $30 millionin 2014 and 2015 respectively.

Progress during the last 12-18 months

PMI provided support to the MOH/MCDMCH, MSL and other stakeholders to improve the collection, management, and use of logistics data through the development of an electronic Logistics Management Information System (eLMIS). In April 2014, the MOH approved the implementation of the eLMIS, an innovative tool which will electronically gather malaria logistics data (e.g., stock on hand, consumption, losses and adjustments) at facilities and transfers data electronically to MSL for order creation.

In 2015, MOH/MCDMCH, with support from partners, rolled out the eLMIS Central version to MSL, CHAZ, and all provincial and district eLMIS end users. This innovation will enable staff to enter logistics data and approve facility orders directly as opposed to submitting forms to MSL. In addition, this will increase central level visibility of stock management at facility level.

---

[7] The MOH, in collaboration with partners, launched the Essential Medicines Logistics Program (EMLIP) in April 2009. This initiative aimed to improve access to essential drugs in the public sector in Zambia. The model eliminated the intermediate storage of drugs at the district level. The district store was converted into a "cross-dock," i.e., point of transit, wherein it receives shipments from MSL that are pre-packed for individual health facilities. In 2014, the MOH with support from partners evaluated EMLIP and redesigned EMLIP to include health center on the list of products to be distributed hence the name EMLIP hybrid.

The eLMIS has now replaced the Supply Chain Manager software previously used for tracking logistics data.

Furthermore, in 2015, the MOH/MCDMCH with support from partners rolled out the redesigned EMLIP hybrid system to 30 additional districts. This brings the total trained to 68 districts (out of 106 districts). It is estimated that rollout of the EMLIP hybrid system will be completed by the end of June 2016.

The Logistcs Management Unit at the MOH recorded a 98% reporting rate and improved commodity facility level stock availability (96%) for malaria commodities in EMLIP districts for the period January to June 2015 of FY 2015. In addition, according to monthly reports sent to the LMU from health facilities, the percentage of health facilities stocked out of all presentations of ACT fell from 5% in June 2014 to 3% in April 2015.

PMI continued to provide support to the national core group led by the MOH/NMCP to conduct annual and biannual forecasting and quantification exercises for ACTs, ITNs, RDTs, and SP. The national core group successfully conducted a transparent forecast and quantification exercise for 2015 through 2017. The entire process was facilitated by MOH/NMCP staff.

To improve strategic management and planning for increased commodity security, PMI provided support to the NMCP Malaria Case Management technical working group. As part of this support, PMI contributed to the finalization of a fully budgeted National Supply Chain Strategy (including an implementation plan). The final strategy has been approved but is yet to be publicly released. Technical assistance was also provided in support of technical organization capacity assessment for MSL in view of its new mandates.

Plans and justification

In collaboration with the MOH, PMI will continue strengthening the GRZ's commodities supply and logistics systems at central, provincial, district, and health center level. PMI will provide support for the continued rollout of EMLIP in collaboration with the MOH to improve the availability of malaria commodities at all levels of the health system. In addition, support will be provided to increase the MOH's ownership and coordination of forecasting, quantification and procurement planning for malaria commodities. PMI will continue to provide support to assess and monitor stock status for antimalarial drugs and RDTs at central, district, and health center levels.

Proposed activities with FY 2016 funding: ($1,099,980)
PMI will assist the MOH in the roll-out of EMLIP hybrid as well as provide technical assistance to strengthen pharmaceutical and supply chain management systems. Specific activities will include the following:

- Provide technical assistance for quarterly forecasting of antimalarial drug and RDT needs and gaps in all districts. ($100,000)

- Provide technical assistance to strengthen the importation, quality control, storage, distribution, and inventory management from central level to the health facility level. (costs included in commodity-specific procurement line items listed above)

- Provide technical assistance to support the rollout of EMLIP including training health workers, monitoring and supportive supervision, improving feedback, and reporting on consumption/stocks from health facility to district and higher levels. ($699,980)

- Support semi-annual end-use verification activities to track the availability of key antimalarial commodities at the facility level. Facilities will be selected to detect ACT (or other drug) stockouts, expiration dates of ACTs at health facilities, leakage, anomalies in ACT use by clinicians, and to verify quantification/consumption assumptions. ($100,000)

- Provide technical assistance to MSL in support of its new mandate to ensure successful adoption of its new tasks, including forecasting and supply planning capacity, as well as the improvement of the storage and distribution of malaria commodities. ($200,000)

5. Health system strengthening and capacity building

PMI supports a broad array of health system strengthening activities which cut across intervention areas, such as training of health workers, supply chain management and health information systems strengthening, drug efficacy monitoring, and NMCP capacity building.

In Zambia, the health portfolio is divided between the Ministry of Health (MOH) and the Ministry of Community Development Mother and Child Health (MCDMCH). Under the new arrangement, the Ministry of Health is responsible for planning, health policy guidelines, surveillance, monitoring and evaluation, allocating funds, and sourcing key health inputs including drugs and equipment for service delivery. The MCDMCH is responsible for providing technical oversight for the implementation of health activities at district, health center, health post, and community levels.

The NMCC is the department under the Directorate of Disease Surveillance and Research of the MOH that provides technical and management oversight to malaria activities in public health facilities to the provincial level, as well as supporting and coordinating a wide range of partners, including research and training institutions. The NMCP has 10 staff positions, including a Case Management Officer; Chief Entomologist; Chief Parasitologist; Malaria Epidemiologist; BCC, IRS, Surveillance and Information, and ITN Officers; Medical Laboratory Technologist; and Operational Research Officer. At the provincial and district level, Provincial Health Offices serve as an extension of the MOH.

The MCDMCH is tasked with service delivery such as implementation of IRS, FANC, ITN distribution, and malaria case management at level 1 hospitals, health centers, and community levels. These activities are implemented through the District Community Medical Offices (DCMO) with NMCC/MOH in the background providing technical but not operational assistance. The DCHO provides overall planning, coordination, and monitoring of malaria

49

activities within their districts. The DCMO have the fiscal authority to manage district health centers and therefore become the main implementers of the IRS program. At the national level, there are four positions within MCDMCH that support the NMCP including a Malaria Specialist, Principal Malaria Control Officer, and Malaria Epidemiologist.

The NMCP staff are committed to scaling-up malaria control and prevention activities; however, they are currently understaffed, and need further support to effectively supervise provincial-level activities and effectively coordinate the many partners contributing to malaria efforts in Zambia. In particular, the NMCP and partners recognize its need for additional coordination of IRS activities and advocacy and outreach efforts. The NMCP requires support to conduct provincial-level visits for supervision and program management which MACEPA and PMI are providing. PMI will support the IRS and SM&E programs. This partner will provide support for IRS training, mapping of households, entomology expertise and assistance for NMCP in gathering and analysis of malaria data. In addition, PMI will work with this partner to provide technical and system support to MCDMCH to standardize the implementation of case reporting by CHWs into the HMIS. PMI also supports capacity building within both NMCC and MCDMCH through the Field Epidemiology Training Program. Currently, one resident is placed at the NMCC and during the next year intermediate residents from the program will be placed at the national, provincial, and district levels to support MCDMCH.

NMCP/PMI objectives

The NMSP vision, goals, and objectives are focused on working towards a malaria free Zambia in 2020. Within the NMSP, there are several strategies designed to work towards this vision. The proposed strategies have been aligned to, and structured along, the "Six Health Systems Building Blocks" framework in order to facilitate a comprehensive analysis. These building blocks include: health service delivery; health workforce; medical products, infrastructure, and equipment; health information; healthcare financing; and leadership and governance. The specific strategies related to this area are as follows:

Health Workforce
1. Improve the availability and distribution of qualified health workers in the country.
2. Significantly increase the annual outputs of the health training institutions in order to mitigate the critical shortages of qualified health workers.

Health Information and Surveillance, Monitoring and Evaluation
1. Strengthen surveillance, monitoring, and evaluation systems in order to ensure timely availability of quality, consistent, and relevant data on malaria control performance to guide policy and decision-making, during the course of this strategic plan.
2. Strengthen operations research to generate evidence to support informed decision-making on policy and implementation of the malaria program.

Progress since PMI was launched

Although there has been an increase in the total reported cases of malaria from 2009 - 2013, the number of reported deaths due to severe malaria has been reduced by 39% (from 5,088 to 3,242). This may be due in part to better case management and possibly increased testing and treatment at the community level. The national HMIS has also been upgraded from the District Health Information System 1.4 to 2.0 (DHIS2), offering significant improvements in timeliness of reporting, data visualization and data systems management. This ability to better utilize data led to alert the NMCP of the deteriorating malaria situation in North-West Province. Zambia historically has high coverage of IPTp and this continues to be the case as the new WHO Guidelines for IPTp are adapted and implemented in-country. PMI trained 504 healthcare workers last year alone in IPTp in the new guidelines which has resulted in maintaining 72% national coverage of at least two doses.

Progress during the last 12-18 months

The PMI Zambia team has been providing technical assistance and capacity building at the NMCP including SM&E, and CHW training in iCCM that together with many other interventions for malaria and other diseases have resulted in a 55% reduction in all-cause mortality rates for children under the age of five (DHS). An example of this impact is evident in the PMI-funded operational research study that showed substantial reductions of inpatient admissions and outpatient visits for malaria after the scale-up of interventions and hospital spending on malaria interventions also decreased by a factor of ten.[8] In addition, PMI used mapping technology, paired with health facility case data, to identify malaria hot spots within districts that were targeted for IRS. This information was coupled with population and structure density data to determine the most cost-effective areas to spray. These routine surveillance activities and targeted surveys are designed move the Zambia public health system towards a data driven culture.

Additionally, PMI funded a malaria focal person at the Zambia WHO Country Office who provided technical support to the drafting team to conduct a comprehensive gap analysis, partner mapping, and the writing of the Transitional Funding Mechanism Global Fund Application and its presentation to the Country Coordinating Committee for endorsement before transmission to the Global Fund Secretariat in Geneva. He provided support for the 2015 MIS and revision of National Malaria Treatment Guidelines.

The PMI and Peace Corps have strengthened their partnership by jointly implementing an ongoing ITN durability monitoring. The Peace Corps Malaria Coordinator in Zambia manages this project. Over 35 Peace Corps volunteers have been engaged at both the provincial and local level within the two provinces where the study is taking place. Additionally, the PMI Resident Advisors provide subject matter expertise to the Peace Corps Malaria Coordinator to train over 250 Peace Corps volunteers in Zambia on malaria.

PMI supported a Field Epidemiology Training Program (FETP) Resident in the first cohort of the program. The resident was assigned to NMCP and conducted a surveillance analysis of malaria incidence rates from 2011 – 2013. In addition, a study is planned to examine the incremental impact of focal indoor residual spraying (fIRS) on incidence of malaria in Mansa District,

---

[8]Comfort, A.B., et al. 2014 Hospitals and Costs Incurred at the Facility Level after scale-up of Malaria Control: Pre-post Comparisons from Two Hospitals in Zambia, American Journal of Tropical Medicine and Hygiene, 90: 20-22.

Luapula Province. FETP is in the process of implementing an intermediate level training in 2015 that will focus on building capacity at the provincial and district levels.

Plans and justification

PMI plans to focus funding from FY 2016 on standardization of reporting at the district and community level, support of national operations research agenda that will identify focus areas to move towards malaria elimination, and creating a culture of data driven decision-making at the national and sub-national level. This will be accomplished through the following activities listed below.

Proposed activities with FY 2016 funding: ($230,000)

- Provide support to strengthen NMCP staff capacity through professional development activities. Activities will include training workshops (e.g., M&E, commodity quantification) and regional/global meetings (e.g., American Society for Tropical Medicine and Hygiene). ($60,000)

- Provide support to enhance national capacity in health systems strengthening, PMI will support the NMCP for HMIS, CHW, and other elements of the public health system in Zambia. (costs included in case management and M&E line items)

- Support for Peace Corps Third Year volunteer. Housing and travel for one Peace Corps volunteer to assist in malaria activities and operational research as a Third Year or Response Volunteer. Provide support for Peace Corps activities including provincial training of trainers courses and small project assistance grants. ($20,000)

- Provide support for two Zambian national to participate in a field epidemiology Training Program either at the intermediate or advanced level. This activity will support long-term local capacity within the MOH. ($150,000)

Table L: Health Systems Strengthening Activities

HSS Building Block	Technical Area	Description of Activity
Health Services	Case Management	Strengthen malaria diagnostic testing, quality assurance, and use at the district and community levels.
Health Workforce	Health Systems Strengthening	Enhance national capacity in health systems strengthening, PMI will support the NMCP for HMIS, CHW, and other elements of the public health system in Zambia
Health Information	Monitoring and Evaluation	Strengthen routine M&E systems (HMIS) at national level and in four targeted provinces. PMI will help strengthen the HMIS at health facility, district, and provincial levels. Implementation activities will include: support for training and supervision of data clerical staff at health facilities and district community health offices including support to DHIS2; improving collection and reporting of routine malaria indicators at community level; and strengthening malaria data analysis and use for planning and decision making
	Operational Research	Provide resources and technical assistance to conduct economic evaluation of interventions, determination of the efficacy of targeted IRS in areas with universal ITN coverage, and examining the impact and cost-effectiveness of targeted IRS
Essential Medical Products, Vaccines, and Technologies	Case Management	Provide technical assistance to support the rollout of EMLIP including training health workers and improving feedback and reporting on consumption/stocks from health facility to district and higher levels

6. Behavior change communication

NMCP/PMI objectives

The most recent NMCP BCC strategy ended in 2014. However, it continues to be in effect until a new strategy document is developed in 2015. The NMCP's BCC strategy for 2011–2014 has clear behavior change objectives for each of the malaria control interventions, and also identifies barriers to the desired behaviors. Target audiences are also identified and measurable communication objectives are clearly stipulated. All institutions working on malaria, including public, private, non-governmental organizations (NGOs), and PMI are required to follow the national strategy. Technical coordination of BCC activities are also conducted through the national BCC TWG as well as a malaria specific BCC TWG.

Progress since PMI was launched

PMI progress on BCC to date has included the development of NMCP's national BCC strategy and training materials used by BCC implementing partners working in malaria prevention and treatment. Case management training for health workers and CHWs has included a BCC component and CHWs are given job aid posters and story boards to conduct sensitization sessions on malaria prevention and treatment in their communities. The national BCC strategy, training materials, and tools are used not only in the PMI target areas, but also by the Global Fund implementers in the remaining areas of the country. PMI has also supported training of NGO staff on BCC related to malaria prevention, and supported Peace Corps volunteers to work with local NGOs on implementing malaria BCC activities in various provinces.

BCC efforts contributed to improved malaria knowledge among Zambians. Knowledge about malaria among women has increased from 2006 to 2012, including: on fever as a cause of malaria (from 65% to 78%), on nets as a malaria prevention method (from 78% to 86%), and on mosquito bites as a cause of malaria (from 80% to 89%). Furthermore, net use among pregnant women and children under age of five has also increased from 2006 to 2012 (from 32% to 62% among pregnant women, and from 32% to 60% among children under five). IPTp coverage among pregnant women increased from 59% in 2006 to 72% in 2012.

Progress during the last 12-18 months

PMI supports several vehicles for its communication activities. PMI has been supporting the implementation of an integrated community-based communications focusing on promotion of malaria prevention, diagnosis, appropriate treatment, and nutrition for pregnant women and children under five in 8 districts and 131 communities across 4 higher malaria burden provinces since 2011. The provinces and districts covered by this activities are: Chipata and Chadiza (Eastern Province), Kasama and Mpulungu (Northern Province), Mansa and Samfya (Luapula Province), and Mongu and Kaoma (Western Province). Community malaria counseling agents went door to door in their communities each week to counsel households on the many ways they can prevent malaria and decrease its impact. At the conclusion of each visit, the agents collected data on every household's behavior the past week; these data shed light on which households were consistently adopting which healthy behaviors. This weekly feedback highlighted the gaps, showcasing where additional support from the counselors was needed. The feedback loop implemented by the partner lead to a 10% increase in regular ITN use compared to communities without a community counseling agents.[9]

PMI has also been supporting technical assistance for the MOH to strengthen malaria BCC by developing and implementing community-level BCC activities, which focus on malaria care seeking and net use. PMI supported training of 3,472 people including Provincial Health Education Officers, District Health Promotion Focal Persons, and individuals and organizations involved in community-based health promotion. The activities included establishing and guiding BCC Coordinating Committees in 40 malaria endemic districts. These committees take responsibility for strengthening BCC coordination and implementation across the district and within communities. PMI also supported strengthening the capacity of community drama groups

---

[9]Communications Support for Health: Final Report 2014

to communicate appropriate malaria messages in an effective manner to increase demand for and utilization of malaria interventions at the district level. The DCMOs also received a training video on community theater, which captures the process of training community drama practitioners and documents the entire process of a community drama session.

In addition, PMI has been supporting BCC activities to prevent malaria during pregnancy through SMAGs. PMI resources complement funding from other with other donors/partners to support these activities. By the end of 2014, the areas covered by SMAGs recorded impressive results, with the proportion of pregnant women who attended antenatal care increasing from 60% to 93% and the proportion of eligible pregnant women who received IPTp increasing from 55% to 95% in the targeted communities. The proportion of persons who had a fever in the past two weeks who got a malaria test increased from 70% to 87% while the proportion of persons who slept under an ITN increased from 48% to 65%.[10] This successful approach will continue to be utilized in similar activities in targeted districts in the future.

As Zambia advances in its control of malaria efforts, the behavioral issues it will encounter will be more and more complex and likely demand further investments to resolve them. Improving coverage of some interventions will likely slow down as early adopters of malaria interventions have already been reached and late adopters require additional and innovative ways to convince them to adopt and maintain the behaviors that, to date, they have rejected. Late adopters may not be homogenously distributed in the population and it will require special efforts to identify and reach them. A PMI-supported formative study and a KAP study are planned for 2015. The two studies will inform development of the new national malaria BCC strategic plan 2015 - 2020.

Plans and justification

A mix of communication activities—mass media, community, and interpersonal—is necessary to inform, promote, and maintain the behaviors to prevent and treat malaria. The mix of activities is dependent on the types of behaviors, barriers to behaviors, and whether the behavior has reached a critical mass in the population. However, in all cases, communication activities need to be sustained or the behavior will change over time, as the risk is perceived to have disappeared.

PMI will support BCC implementation for malaria in four target provinces (Luapula, Northern, Eastern, and Muchinga Provinces) at health facility and community levels through community mobilization and community dialogues. This will lead to increased acceptance of IRS, increased ANC attendance with higher IPTp uptake, and improved health care seeking behavior and increased demand for and acceptance of malaria diagnostics. At the national level, PMI will support the NMCP for malaria focused BCC strategies and materials in collaboration with other partners.

---

[10] Community Household Monitoring Report: Communications Support for Health (CSH) Program (2014).

Proposed activities with FY 2016 funding: ($1,500,000)

The NMCP believes that both national and community BCC activities are needed to change and maintain behaviors in malaria prevention and treatment. Each approach reaches different audiences and reinforces key messages. The final mix of mass, community, and interpersonal communication activities and technical orientation will be based on evidence that will help focus efforts. A part of the M&E strategy for BCC will be to analyze information collected through the regular MIS about knowledge and practices, as well coverage estimates (i.e., final results of BCC efforts). Emphasis will be to maintain current levels of coverage and expand to cohorts that have been difficult to reach or are recalcitrant in adopting the desired behaviors. The list below provides potential tasks and their rationale:

- Conduct national mass media and other BCC activities to:
  - maintain ownership and proper use of ITNs through national multi-media efforts. National activities will focus on at least three groups: first, maintenance of appropriate behaviors in the population that is already exhibiting them; second, introduction of new cohorts to the desired behaviors; and, third reaching late adopters and those who are difficult to reach geographically ($150,000);
  - increase ANC attendance and demand for IPTp. National BCC efforts for malaria in pregnancy are part of a larger integrated campaign on maternal health and nutrition that disseminates messages through national radio and television spots ($150,000); and
  - increase early care-seeking behavior for fevers and demand for malaria diagnosis. Mass media activities will promote early care seeking actions in health facilities, awareness of and demand for proper malaria diagnosis, and adherence to the treatment of malaria cases ($150,000).

- Conduct community-based BCC in four targeted provinces through NGOs/faith-based organizations to:
  - increase net ownership and correct and consistent use of ITNs. Primary focus will be to target late adopters require a more focused and interpersonal approach ($350,000);
  - increase ANC attendance and demand for IPTp. BCC activities through community groups (SMAGs) will be implemented to increase use of IPTp ($350,000); and
  - increase early care-seeking behavior for fevers and demand for malaria diagnosis usage at the community-level ($350,000).

7. Monitoring and evaluation

NMCP/PMI objectives

The revised Zambia NMSP 2011–2016 states the objective of SM&E is to: "strengthen SM&E systems in order to ensure timely availability of quality, consistent and relevant data on malaria

control performance by 2016." These data guide policy and decision-making. Along with the revised NMSP, a revised National M&E Plan will be developed to address the challenges in Zambia as it moves along malaria's epidemiological continuum. The M&E strategy tracks all Roll Back Malaria-recommended indicators. Three SM&E strategies are:
1. Strengthen coordination/collaboration in surveillance, monitoring and evaluation
2. Data management systems—strengthen the implementation of data management systems at community, facility, district, provincial, and national levels to efficiently collect, process, analyze, and manage malaria transmission and disease data
3. Surveillance to track progress towards elimination—strengthen capacities of health personnel at all levels with the aim of improving quality and timeliness of case detection and reporting

PMI's support to M&E in Zambia aligns with the NMSP and the National Malaria M&E Plan. PMI coordinates and collaborates with the NMCP and several partners in providing technical assistance and resources for M&E activities including MACEPA, the Global Fund, UNICEF, and WHO.

Progress since PMI was launched

Surveillance and monitoring: As of 2013, the national HMIS has been upgraded from the District Health Information System (DHIS) 1.4 to 2.0 in all districts throughout the country. Malaria cases are reported through the National HMIS using a combination of paper tools and the DHIS2 with all public and mission health facilities and some private facilities reporting health data monthly through the HMIS. Information flows from the health facility to the district and provincial level before being transmitted to the HMIS group within the MOH. The NMCP accesses malaria data from the MOH HMIS and maintains its own web-based data management system using the DHIS2 platform. The HMIS collects data on malaria clinical and confirmed cases, OPD, and inpatient cases, and deaths by age under one year, one to five years, and over five years.

Evaluation: To evaluate outcomes and impact of malaria prevention and control activities in Zambia, nationally-representative surveys such as the DHS and the MIS are performed periodically. All-cause mortality in children under five years of age is tracked using the DHS; other child health indicators are also collected by the DHS and used in assessing impact. The 2007 DHS report provides a baseline estimate of mortality at the start of PMI. The 2014 DHS is complete and the final report is available.

Nationwide MISs were carried out in 2006, 2008, 2010, and 2012 to provide information on the coverage of the four major malaria interventions, malaria parasite prevalence, and the prevalence of severe anemia, which is useful for measuring changes over time. The most recent MIS occurred in 2015 and a preliminary report is expected in early 2016.

A number of other non-PMI-financed surveys and evaluations provide additional provincial-, district-, and community-level data on malaria epidemiology in Zambia, and provide useful information on the progress of malaria control efforts. These include health facility surveys to assess health worker performance and the quality of health care; availability of health guidelines, personnel, and equipment; and household surveys to assess knowledge, attitudes, and practices related to malaria. As part of routine supervisory visits to MOH facilities, checklists are also completed on health worker performance and other technical aspects of health care. Table L shows household and facility surveys implemented and planned from 2010 to 2018.

Progress during the last 12-18 months

HMIS: At the national level, DHIS 2 provides significant improvements in timeliness of reporting, data visualization, and data systems management. Capacity building activities have been conducted at all levels of the health system in surveillance, monitoring, and evaluation. According to WHO, in 2013 the reporting rate for health facilities was 90%, with 20,124 reports out of 22,308 total expected (1,859 facilities x 12 months). The DHIS2 platform allows for data to be analyzed using maps, charts, pivot tables, or summarized through dashboards. Malaria data from the HMIS are being used to follow trends in incidence at the district level, targeting health facility catchment areas for IRS, locating hot spots in very low endemic areas, and following trends in confirmed cases and diagnostic use.

Rapid Reporting: Malaria surveillance systems were developed for Southern Province at the facility level using the malaria rapid reporting system, mobile phones, and geographic information system. Health care workers report malaria cases, lab testing, and drug availability by web-enabled cell phones on a weekly basis. These data can be accessed through DHIS2 online platform. This rapid reporting system has been expanded to additional facilities in Western and Central Provinces.

Active Infection Detection: The previously PMI-supported enhanced surveillance in Lusaka District has been transitioned over to the Lusaka District Health Office. Active infection detection is ongoing in 23 of the 28 district health facilities. Community-level malaria reactive case detection continues in very low prevalence areas in Southern Province.

End-Use Verification: The EUV collects data on malaria commodities every month from facilities to assess availability. The last report for EUV is for the first quarter of 2015. The data reported is from 42 health facilities visited in February 2015. Over 33% of facilities had all four AL presentations and there was only one facility with no ACTs available. Most facilities (68%– 100%) were appropriately stocked with malaria commodities; none were overstocked. The index of ACT availability, shown in Figure 8, confirms small improvements from fisrt quarter 2013 to 2015. The 2015 EUV reports only one facility with an RDT stockout.

Figure 8: Index of AL availability in health facilities, EUV, 1st Quarter 2013 (23 facilities), 2014 (11 facilities), and 2015 (42 facilities)

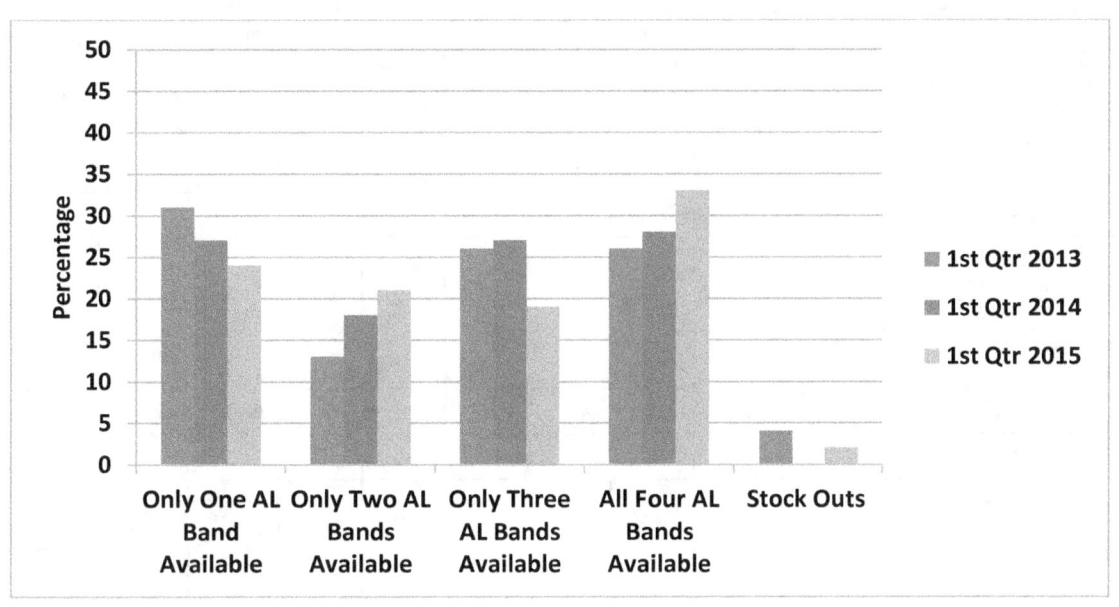

Note: each band is a dose packet size.
Source: End Use Verification report, 1st Quarter 2013, 2014, and 2015

Table M. Monitoring and Evaluation Data Sources

Data Source	Survey Activities	Year								
		2010	2011	2012	2013	2014	2015	2016	2017	2018
National-level Household surveys	Demographic Health Survey (DHS)					X				(X)*
	Malaria Indicator Survey (MIS)	X		X			X			(X)
	EPI survey		X							
Health Facility and Other Surveys	School-based malaria survey									
	Health facility survey		X				X*	(X)		
	SPA survey									
	EUV survey	X	X	X	X	X	X	(X)	(X)	(X)
	KAP survey						(X)			
Malaria Surveillance and Routine System Support	Support to malaria surveillance system					X*	X*	(X)*	(X)*	(X)*
	Electronic Logistics Management Information System (eLMIS)					X	X	(X)	(X)	(X)
	Support to HMIS/DHIS2				X*	X*	X	(X)	(X)	(X)
Therapeutic Efficacy monitoring	In vivo efficacy testing			X	X	X	X		(X)	
Entomology	Entomological surveillance and resistance monitoring		X*	X	X	X	X	(X)	(X)	(X)
Other malaria-related evaluations	Malaria Program Review	X			X					
Other Data Sources	Malaria Impact Evaluation					X*				
*Not PMI-funded ( ) Planned activity										

Plans and justification

Monitoring and evaluating malaria prevention and control activities will rely on a combination of routine malaria data through the HMIS and surveys. With FY 2016 funds, PMI will provide support to strengthen routine malaria data collection at the community, health facility, district, provincial, and national levels through the HMIS. The objective is to achieve 100% on-time reporting of malaria cases by districts and 90% by health facilities in PMI-targeted provinces. PMI will ensure the SM&E activities at the national level and in the four PMI-supported provinces are complementary. In the following fiscal year (FY 2017), PMI will consider providing support for a national household survey conducted in 2018. With FY 2016 funds, PMI will support the following activities:

Proposed activities with FY 2016 funding: ($1,400,000)

- Strengthen routine M&E systems (HMIS) at national level and in four targeted high burden provinces. PMI will help strengthen the HMIS at health facility, district, and provincial levels. Implementation activities will include: support for training of data clerical staff at health facilities and district community health offices to correctly perform all aspects related to collecting and reporting HMIS data and in using DHIS2 and support HMIS supervision, and monitoring and mentoring visits; improving collection and reporting of routine malaria indicators at community level; and strengthening malaria data analysis and use for planning and decision making. ($500,000)

- Provide resources for central-level NMCP personnel to conduct and follow up on data quality audits in all districts and provincial offices in one year. This activity entails visiting officers responsible for collecting, collating, and reporting data from health facilities to higher levels of the health system and ensuring that appropriate quality procedures are followed. No other donors are currently funding this activity. ($100,000)

- Support national-level M&E activities, including HMIS strengthening, national-level coordination with partners such as MACEPA, the EU, etc. for their M&E activities, support M&E technical working group meetings, provide technical assistance to enhance standardization and reporting of national, facility, and community-level data. ($600,000)

- Monitor durability of ITNs following mass campaign. ($180,000)

- Provide CDC technical assistance for routine monitoring of net durability. ($10,000)

- Provide CDC technical assistance in monitoring and evaluation activities. ($10,000)

8. Operational research (OR)

The NMCP in Zambia has many ongoing and planned research activities with a number of different partners. In FY 2015 PMI supported the NMCP to develop an Operational Research Agenda to better map out current and future operations research activities and goals. This will be used to help coordinate current research activities and for planning purposes to align future research activities with the goals of the NMCP.

Completed OR studies

PMI supported an operational research project on ITN durability that was completed in 2013 (see ITN section). This study examining structural integrity of ITNs distributed in Northern and Luapula Provinces was started in 2011 and the field work was completed by the end of 2013. The data showed a lack of increase in total hole area as nets aged and suggested that this is likely due to ITN attrition that might occur between two and three-and-a-half years. At 27 - 30 months,

ITNs already had a large total hole surface area that was equivalent to the oldest nets observed. Nets were often tucked under reed mats which may explain the finding that the largest hole area was found in the lower half of the net.[11] Additionally, a PMI-funded study of the efficacy of SP for IPTp in Mansa, Zambia was completed in 2013. (see the MIP section for more information.)

Ongoing OR studies

Association between malaria control scale-up and micro-economic outcomes: evidence from a retrospective analysis in Zambia:

While substantial attention has been devoted to understanding the effectiveness of malaria control strategies on health outcomes, there has been less focus on understanding the economic impact of malaria control interventions. As malaria control interventions are scaled up and malaria episodes decrease, households may experience economic benefits such as improved household income and consumption, worker productivity, schooling attendance, and poverty status. This study assesses the associations between malaria control scale-up and micro-economic indicators in Zambia, where significant progress has been made in scaling up effective malaria control strategies, but also where malaria continues to be an important public health concern. Using data from 2006 to 2010 on the distribution of ITNs and IRS, this study examines whether the scale-up of these activities in Zambia is associated with improved micro-economic outcomes at the household level. Specifically, the study will try to determine whether or not these activities affect household spending on food, household spending on medical care, schooling attendance, agricultural production, and household savings and borrowing.

Impact and cost-effectiveness of focal IRS with pirimiphos-methyl in Nchelenge District: Identifying targeting strategies to maximize protection while minimizing cost

This study started during the 2014–2015 IRS campaign and will assess the impact and cost-effectiveness of focal IRS with pirimiphos-methyl in Nchelenge District through measurement of changes in parasite prevalence, vector density, and insecticide resistance in areas targeted for spraying, neighboring communities and distant communities. The main goal is to identify optimal strategies to target IRS guided by readily available data on population demographics, malaria epidemiology, vector bionomics and ecological characteristics that can be implemented throughout Zambia. The study will: a) Measure the impact of focal IRS with pirimiphos-methyl in Nchelenge District on the number of confirmed malaria cases presenting to health facilities, parasite prevalence, vector density and insecticide resistance; b) Measure the cost-effectiveness of focal IRS with pirimiphos-methyl in Nchelenge District; and c) Identify demographic, epidemiological, entomological, and ecological factors associated with the effectiveness of focal IRS with pirimiphos-methyl in Nchelenge District.

---

[11] Long-lasting insecticidal nets in Zambia: a cross-sectional analysis of net integrity and insecticide content Allen S. Craig*, Mbanga Muleba, Stephen C. Smith, Cecilia Katebe-Sakala, Gershom Chongwe, Busiku Hamainza, Batuke Walusiku, Megan Tremblay, Maureen Oscadal, Robert Wirtz and Kathrine R. Tan *Malaria Journal* 2015, 14:239

Planned OR studies

A recent policy change in Zambia now emphasizes universal coverage of ITNs with targeted IRS. Historically, vector control was split, with IRS reserved for urban and peri-urban areas while ITNs were targeted to rural areas. This approach in vector control has been ineffective, leading to increases in malaria cases in several districts throughout the country.

The new approach to vector control may be more cost-effective and ultimately could have a greater impact on malaria control and prevention in Zambia. Unfortunately, little data exist to help drive the decision-making process of determining where IRS would be best targeted in combination with universal ITN coverage. The OR study proposed would help shed light on this issue in Zambia. It will also contribute to the limited scientific body of knowledge regarding the added benefit of IRS in combination with ITNs. This will be a second phase of the ongoing study—*Impact and cost-effectiveness of focal IRS with pirimiphos-methyl in Nchelenge District: Identifying targeting strategies to maximize protection while minimizing cost.* The second phase is designed to provide information that would guide implementation of the proposed policy change by NMCP. The study seeks to provide an evidence base for the designing focal IRS campaigns capable of delivering maximum impact to areas of high transmission. By matching IRS impact to parasite prevalence and mosquito vector abundance, the cost-effectiveness of two focal IRS strategies in reducing parasite prevalence will be measured. The primary outcome will be parasite prevalence by PCR. Secondary outcomes will include parasite prevalence by RDT, anopheline mosquito density per household, insecticide resistance profiles, and cost effectiveness.

Table N: Summary of Operations Research

Completed OR Studies			
Title	**Start Date**	**End Date**	**Budget**
The efficacy of SP for IPTp, Mansa, Zambia	January 2010	Published June 2014	$200,000
ITN prospective durability study	2011		$50,000
Ongoing OR Studies			
Title	**Start Date**	**End Date**	**Budget**
Association between malaria control scale-up and micro-economic outcomes: evidence from a retrospective analysis in Zambia	December 2014	October 2015	$220,000
Impact and cost-effectiveness of focal IRS with pirimiphos-methyl in Nchelenge District: Identifying targeting strategies to maximize protection while minimizing cost	December 2014	December 2016	$324,299
Planned OR Studies			
Title	**Start Date**	**End Date**	**Budget**
Targeted IRS with long-lasting ITNs study	2016 (pending approval)		$300,000

Proposed activities with FY 2016 funding: ($320,000)

- PMI will support operational research activity to determine the efficacy of targeted IRS in areas with universal ITN coverage. ($300,000)

- PMI is supporting operational research in Zambia that will help clarify several important issues. CDC will provide two technical assistance visits to support the ongoing OR. ($20,000)

9. Staffing and administration

Two health professionals serve as resident advisors to oversee PMI in Zambia, one representing CDC and one representing USAID. In addition, one or more Foreign Service Nationals (FSNs) work as part of the PMI team. All PMI staff members are part of a single interagency team led by the USAID Mission Director or his/her designee in country. The PMI team shares responsibility for development and implementation of PMI strategies and work plans, coordination with national authorities, managing collaborating agencies and supervising day-to-day activities. Candidates for resident advisor positions (whether initial hires or replacements) will be evaluated and/or interviewed jointly by USAID and CDC, and both agencies will be involved in hiring decisions, with the final decision made by the individual agency.

The PMI professional staff work together to oversee all technical and administrative aspects of the PMI, including finalizing details of the project design, implementing malaria prevention and treatment activities, monitoring and evaluation of outcomes and impact, reporting of results, and providing guidance to PMI partners.

The PMI lead in country is the USAID Mission Director. The day-to-day lead for PMI is delegated to the USAID Health Office Director and thus the two PMI resident advisors, one from USAID and one from CDC, report to the USAID Health Office Director for day-to-day leadership, and work together as a part of a single interagency team. The technical expertise housed in Atlanta and Washington guides PMI programmatic efforts.

The two PMI resident advisors are based within the USAID health office and are expected to spend approximately half their time sitting with and providing technical assistance to the national malaria control programs and partners.

Locally-hired staff to support PMI activities either in Ministries or in USAID will be approved by the USAID Mission Director. Because of the need to adhere to specific country policies and USAID accounting regulations, any transfer of PMI funds directly to Ministries or host governments will need to be approved by the USAID Mission Director and Controller, in addition to the U.S. Global Malaria Coordinator.

Proposed activities with FY 2016 funding: ($1,133,520)

- Support for in-country PMI staff including one USAID PMI resident advisor with support encompassing salaries, benefits, travel, and other staff support related costs. In addition, support is provided for general administrative costs that enables Mission-wide assistance from which PMI benefits. ($688,244)

- Support for in-country PMI CDC resident advisor with support encompassing salaries, benefits, travel, and other staff support related costs. ($445,276).

Table 1: Budget Breakdown by Mechanism

President's Malaria Initiative – Zambia

Planned Malaria Obligations for FY 2016

Mechanism	Geographic Area	Activity	Budget ($)	%
TBD - Supply Chain Contract	National	Procurement of ACTs, RDTs, nets, provide technical assistance to strengthen pharmaceutical and supply chain systems	9,142,980	38.1%
AIRS	Targeted Districts	Procurement of insecticides for IRS. Support for environmental monitoring and insecticide resistance monitoring	8,294,500	34.6%
TBD - Malaria Bilateral	National and Four Target Provinces (Luapula, Northern, Eastern and Muchinga)	At the national level and in four target districts, improve the quality of parasitological diagnosis in the public sector, strengthen FANC, community-based BCC, roll out additional continuous ITN distribution channels in selected districts, technical assistance to strengthen HMIS	3,880,000	16.2%
TBD - BCC Bilateral	National	Support for national level BCC activities	450,000	1.9%
MalariaCare	National	Strengthen malaria diagnostic capacity and quality assurance nationally through the training of malaria microscopists and support for OTSS.	400,000	1.7%
TBD - Operations Research	TBD	OR for IRS	300,000	1.3%

NMCP	NA	District and provincial data audits, M&E, support for health facility survey	160,000	0.7%
Peace Corps	NA	Support for third year volunteer, provincial training of trainers and small project assistance grants	20,000	0.1%
USAID Staff	NA	Personnel	688,244	2.9%
CDC Staf	NA	Personnel	445,276	1.9%
CDC -IAA	NA	Entomologic monitoring and insecticide resistance monitoring, M&E, net durability monitoring, operations research and FETP	219,000	0.9%
Total			**24,000,000**	**100%**

Table 2: Budget Breakdown by Activity

President's Malaria Initiative – Zambia
Planned Malaria Obligations for FY 2016

Proposed Activity	Mechanism	Budget Total $	Commodity $	Geographic Area	Description
PREVENTIVE ACTIVITIES					
Insecticide-treated Nets					
Procurement of ITNs	TBD – Supply Chain Contract	3,213,000	3,213,000	National	Procure 900,000 ITNs for 2017 mass distribution campaign
Distribution of ITNs	TBD – Supply Chain Contract	500,000		National	Support the distribution of ITNs, including transportation and other logistics, to districts and health facilities.
Provide technical assistance to expand continuous distribution through schools and community	TBD – Malaria Bilateral	150,000		Luapula, Northern, Eastern, and Muchinga	Technical assistance to roll out innovative approaches for ITNs distribution in selected provinces/districts
SUBTOTAL ITNs		**3,863,000**	**3,213,000**		
Indoor Residual Spraying					
Procurement of IRS commodities and support to other components of the program.	AIRS	6,170,500	6,170,500	36 Districts	Procure insecticides and other IRS supplies/equipment for spraying up to 450,000

Proposed Activity	Mechanism	Budget		Geographic Area	Description
		Total $	Commodity $		
					structures. Support environmental monitoring and environmental assessment.
Implementation of IRS program, monitoring and evaluation, storage/incinerator, community sensitization, geocoding, BCC	AIRS	1,674,000		36 Districts	Training, monitoring and evaluation, and BCC for IRS; pesticide storage, waste disposal.
Entomological monitoring and insecticide resistance monitoring and support to insectary	AIRS	450,000		NA	Support insectary and entomological monitoring
CDC technical assistance on entomological monitoring and insecticide resistance	CDC - IAA	29,000		NA	Provide technical assistance on entomological monitoring and insecticide resistance.
SUBTOTAL IRS		**8,323,500**	**6,170,500**		
Malaria in Pregnancy					
Strengthening FANC for IPTp	TBD - Malaria Bilateral	300,000		National and Luapula, Northern, Eastern, and Muchinga	Provide support to train provincial and district level health workers in updated IPTp guidelines in four target high malaria burden provinces (Luapula, Muchinga, Northern, and Eastern)
SUBTOTAL MIP		**300,000**			

Proposed Activity	Mechanism	Budget		Geographic Area	Description
		Total $	Commodity $		
SUBTOTAL PREVENTIVE		**12,486,500**	**9,383,500**		
CASE MANAGEMENT					
Diagnosis and Treatment					
Procurement of RDTs	TBD - Supply Chain Contract	960,000	960,000	National	Procure 3,000,000 RDTs for health facilities and iCCM
Strengthen malaria diagnostic capabilities at the health center level	MalariaCare	400,000		National	Strengthen malaria diagnostic capacity and quality assurance nationally through the training of malaria microscopists and support for OTSS
Improve the quality of parasitological diagnosis in the public sector for four provinces	TBD - Malaria Bilateral	400,000		Luapula, Northern, Eastern, and Muchinga	Training and Supportive Supervision of healthcare providers at PHC and community levels to improve the appropriate use of diagnostics
Procure microscopes	TBD - Supply Chain Contract	40,000	40,000	National	Procure microscopes
Procure reagents and supplies	TBD - Supply Chain Contract	30,000	30,000	National	Procure reagents and supplies for microscopy
Procurement of ACTs	TBD - Supply Chain Contract	3,300,000	3,300,000	National	Procure ACTs (artemether-lumefantrine) for the treatment of malaria in facilities and communities and procure injectable artesunate to support the rollout of injectable artesunate in line with

Proposed Activity	Mechanism	Budget Total $	Commodity $	Geographic Area	Description
					updated national malaria case management guidelines
Strengthen facility- and community-based treatment with ACTs	TBD - Malaria Bilateral	700,000		Luapula, Northern, Eastern, and Muchinga	Training, supervision support, to improve service delivery in health facilities including treatment of malaria, and to assist with roll-out into communities through CHWs. Train health workers in new guidelines.
SUBTOTAL DIAGNOSIS AND TREATMENT		**5,830,000**	**4,330,000**		
Pharmaceutical Management					
Roll out the national logistics and pharmaceutical management system for malaria commodities	TBD - Supply Chain Contract	$1,099,980		National	Strengthen supply chain and logistics for all malaria commodities and essential drugs, including Pharmaceutical Regulatory Authority and the end-use verification tool
SUBTOTAL PHARMACEUTICAL MANAGEMENT		**$1,099,980**			
SUBTOTAL CASE MANAGEMENT		**$6,929,980**			
HEALTH SYSTEM STRENGTHENING / CAPACITY BUILDING					
Training and travel to build capacity of NMCP staff	NMCP	60,000		National	Fund travel and registration to international meetings such as MIM, SARN, and

Proposed Activity	Mechanism	Budget Total $	Commodity $	Geographic Area	Description
					ASTMH and regional trainings. Support strategy development.
Peace Corps		20,000		National	Support for third year volunteer, provincial training of trainers and small project assistance grants
Field Epidemiology Training Program	CDC - IAA	150,000		National	Training for one Zambian national in field epidemiology
SUBTOTAL HSS & CAPACITY BUILDING		**230,000**			
BEHAVIOR CHANGE COMMUNICATION					
National BCC to maintain ownership and proper use of ITNs, increase ANC attendance and demand for IPTp, increase early care seeking behavior and demand for proper malaria diagnosis and increased adherence to treatment for malaria	TBD - BCC Bilateral	450,000		National	BCC for proper and consistent net usage, increased ANC attendance and demand for IPTp, and increased early care-seeking behavior and demand for proper malaria diagnosis and adherence to treatment for malaria at national level
Community-based BCC through NGOs/FBOs to increase net ownership and use, increase ANC attendance and demand for increase ANC IPTp, increased early care	TBD - Malaria Bilateral	1,050,000		Luapula, Northern, Eastern, and Muchinga	BCC for proper and consistent net usage, increased ANC attendance and demand for IPTp, and increased early care seeking behavior and demand for proper malaria diagnosis

Proposed Activity	Mechanism	Budget Total $	Commodity $	Geographic Area	Description
seeking behavior and demand for proper malaria diagnosis and adherence to treatment for malaria at national level					and adherence to treatment for malaria at community level
SUBTOTAL BCC		**1,500,000**			
MONITORING AND EVALUATION					
Technical assistance to strengthen HMIS	TBD - Malaria Bilateral	500,000		National	Technical assistance to strengthen HMIS
District and provincial data audits	NMCP	100,000			Resources for central level personnel to conduct and follow up data quality audits all districts and provincial offices
Technical assistance to enhance standardization and reporting of national, facility, and community-level data	TBD - Malaria Bilateral	600,000		Luapula, Northern, Eastern, and Muchinga	Technical assistance to enhance standardization and reporting of national, facility and community-level data
Routine monitoring of net durability	TBD - Malaria Bilateral	180,000		TBD	Routine monitoring of net durability
Technical assistance for routine monitoring of nets	CDC - IAA	10,000		NA	Technical assistance for routine monitoring of nets
Technical assistance for M&E	CDC - IAA	10,000		NA	Technical assistance on monitoring and evaluation issues
SUBTOTAL M&E		**1,400,000**			
OPERATIONS RESEARCH					

Proposed Activity	Mechanism	Budget		Geographic Area	Description
		Total $	Commodity $		
OR – IRS	TBD	300,000		TBD	OR to determine efficacy of targeted IRS in areas with universal ITN coverage
Technical assistance for OR	CDC - IAA	20,000		N/A	Technical assistance for OR
SUBTOTAL OR		320,000			
IN-COUNTRY STAFFING AND ADMINISTRATION					
USAID		688,244			
CDC		445,276			
SUBTOTAL IN-COUNTRY STAFFING		1,133,520			
GRAND TOTAL		$24,000,000	$13,713,500